MANAGING NEW ENTERPRISES

MANAGING NEW ENTERPRISES

Donald Grunewald

Mellen Studies in Business
Volume 19

The Edwin Mellen Press
Lewiston•Queenston•Lampeter

Library of Congress Cataloging-in-Publication Data

Grunewald, Donald.
   Managing new enterprises / Donald Grunewald.
     p. cm. -- (Mellen studies in business ; 19)
   Includes bibliographical references and index.
   ISBN-0-7734-7150-2
     1. New business enterprises--Management. 2. Small business--Management. I. Title.
II. Series.

   HD62.5 .G78 2002
   658.1'1--dc21

                                                  2002072239

This is volume 19 in the continuing series
Mellen Studies in Business
Volume 19 ISBN 0-7734-7150-2
MSB Series ISBN 0-88946-152-X

A CIP catalog record for this book is available from the British Library.

The Edwin Mellen Press
Box 450
Lewiston, New York
USA 14092-0450

The Edwin Mellen Press
Box 67
Queenston, Ontario
CANADA L0S 1L0

The Edwin Mellen Press, Ltd.
Lampeter, Ceredigion, Wales
UNITED KINGDOM SA48 8LT

Printed in the United States of America

DEDICATION

This book is dedicated to a number of entrepreneurs who have touched my life:

LAWRENCE C. DURHAM, *my brother, who established a number of new enterprises in home and interior design.*

P.J. DURHAM, *my step grandfather, who established two businesses in automotive and aviation electrical parts and who established a hotel.*

TINA DURHAM, *my mother, who established a successful real estate brokerage business.*

HARRY A. GRUNEWALD, *my father, who established a chain of restaurants and newsstands in bus stations.*

THEODORE GRUNEWALD, *my cousin, who established an advertising agency and a real estate brokerage business, and who has been involved in many successful new enterprises.*

This book is also dedicated to all entrepreneurs and future entrepreneurs.

TABLE OF CONTENTS

PREFACE

by Joseph O'Donoghue, Ph.D., Fulbright Scholar (Japan, 1980-1981;
Ireland, 1995-1996) Fulbright Scholar Nominee, Ireland 2002-2003)

Readers of this book by Dr. Donald Grunewald can expect to be delighted by his break with the long overworked format in publications dealing with success in entrepreneurship. Grunewald is the total realist who opts for a comprehensive but truncated review of the major problems confronted by the typical U.S. entrepreneur.

Grunewald, the realist, never insults the intelligence of his readers by a myriad of hero-centered, over-hyped, accounts of entrepreneurial star performers. This gives his book a rare and very valuable focus on the ultimate essentials of entrepreneur efforts.

Grunewald divides entrepreneurial activity into seventeen topic areas with each area covered in a single tightly framed chapter. The focus is always on (1) the full range of questions which a reader could be expected to raise on being introduced to a set of problems, and (2) the succinctly stated principles which Grunewald offers as the solution to the problems raised.

An early chapter on the desired personal qualifications of an entrepreneur is a perfect example of Grunewald's skill in downsizing his analysis to the absolute essentials. By this tightness in expression, he is able to target two somewhat different backgrounds in his readers: the about-to-start entrepreneur will find a carefully developed listing of the personal characteristics vital to success as an entrepreneur, while the established entrepreneur will derive a new set of insights into those personal attributes which must now be constantly developed en route to further success as an entrepreneur.

Grunewald also gives early attention to what he regards as the essential process to follow in developing the art of handling money. The chapter is loaded with gentle, but dire, warnings on the range of mistakes that can emerge when skills in the art of money handling remain undeveloped. These mistakes are usually very small in size when they first appear, but Grunewald systematically offers details on how their repetition will ultimately destroy the firm.

In later chapters on the use of capital and the art of debt management Grunewald continues to demonstrate his skill in serving as a mentor to entrepreneurs at different phases of their development, viz., the start-up and the time-to-expand performer. Anyone who reviews the literature on entrepreneurs knows that it is very easy to obtain a book with a helpful listing of sources of capital, plus the usual advice on how to pursue the private and public sources of funding for new firms. Grunewald provides extensive coverage of these multiple sources of funding. His main service to readers, however, is his review of the long-term consequences of the specific choices made by entrepreneurs in regard to the funding pattern they select.

This type of long-term analysis, with all options defined and considered in terms of ultimate consequences, is one of the great advantages of Grunewald's book. This reviewer rarely sees a book on entrepreneurship which directly attacks, in Grunewald fashion, the major challenge to every successful, first growth phase completed, entrepreneurial firm in the U.S: How does the firm break through the one million dollar barrier?

It is not difficult to start a business in the U.S., which is one of the most entrepreneur-friendly nations in the world. Although the dead-after-one-year rate for new start-up firms is a horrendous forty percent, and the dead after ten years rate is an even more horrendous ninety percent, these casualty rates do not reflect the second-try and third-try successes of individual entrepreneurs or family businesses with one or two earlier failures. America, after all, is far more than the land of opportunity; for entrepreneurs it is the land of second, third, and sometimes fourth opportunity on the way to eventual success. The real challenge, and the ultimate challenge, for all U.S. entrepreneurs is to crash through to a business level beyond one million dollars in annual sales. Less than four percent of U.S. entrepreneurs reach this level of success.

Why? Perhaps the key blockage to success beyond one million dollars is the absence of analysis of entrepreneurial analysis by each detail: here are the essential patterns of a Donald Grunewald. It should be very clear by now that the hero-heavy, stereotype-driven, anecdotal-focused approach to entrepreneurial analysis has provided no service to the ninety six percent of all entrepreneurs currently trapped below the million mark, despite all their best efforts to clear that barrier.

Grunewald's book offers an alternative growth path to the over fourteen million small businesses whose leaders have been searching, at a ninety-six percent failure rate, for a path to growth beyond the one million level of sales. One strategy in this regard could be quite simple, but could have enormous impact. Grunewald's seventeen chapters could easily become the focus of discussion at seventeen seminars, held over a period of a year and attended by each and every employee of the nation's almost fifteen million businesses with annual sales below one million dollars. Three or four employees, randomly selected in advance of each seminar, could be the leaders of a discussion on each of Grunewald's chapters, which, of course, would be required reading by all members of the firm prior to each seminar. The entire book could be covered within a one year period, based on one seminar per month plus a five-seminar annual company retreat.

This reevaluation strategy, based on a core document of excellence in analysis, might present ego problems for some of the leaders of entrepreneurial firms. Grunewald is blunt, beautifully blunt, in topic chapters such as "On Being a Good Boss" or "Progressivism," which is his title for a discussion on the root sources of the power to expand a business. But unlike the gurus who, with no measurable impact now provide such services, either in person, at seminars, or in book format, Grunewald does not deliver their product. Grunewald's book is a break-it-down, look-at-the-pieces, forget-the-hype, and forget-the-entrepreneur-stars approach to what works and what does not work in everyday entrepreneurship.

Managing New Enterprises is one person's gift to entrepreneur success based on his own lifetime of review and analysis. Let's hope we all have the wisdom to use his gift.

ACKNOWLEDGEMENTS

I would like to acknowledge the time, effort, and useful advice given by a number of persons to help me complete this book.

First of all, I would like to acknowledge the support and help of academic colleagues at the Hagan School of Business of Iona College. I especially acknowledge the support of the Dean of the Hagan School of Business, Nicholas J. Beutell, Ph.D. I thank my colleagues in the Department of Management and in other departments of the Hagan School of Business at Iona College for their support.

The extensive support of the entire staff of my publisher, The Edwin Mellen Press, is gratefully acknowledged. In particular, I wish to acknowledge the helpful advice and support of Mr. John Rupnow, the Director of The Edwin Mellen Press and of Mrs. Patricia Schultz, the Production Manager of The Edwin Mellen Press.

I am very grateful to Ms. Judie Szuets for her editorial help and for her producing the final two drafts of this book.

I wish to acknowledge the special help of Dr. Joseph O'Donoghue, Fulbright scholar and academic colleague during more than a decade of working together at Mercy College, and for his support and advice since those years, who has written the Preface for this book and who has helped with his suggestions and his review of the book for the publisher. I also thank Dr. Edward C. Yang, President of the John Dewey Foundation, for reviewing the book for the publisher and for his inspiration and helpful advice.

I take full responsibility for any errors or omissions in this book. I am grateful to the many entrepreneurs and others who helped encourage me with their suggestions and support to write this book. I also appreciate the kindness of those who have decided to read this book. I hope it will be useful to all who read it. If any reader has any comments, suggestions, or requests for help, please contact me at my postal address: 5 River Road #307, Wilton, CT 06897 or at dgrune34@aol.com.

1

An Introduction to Entrepreneurship

Entrepreneurship is a creative human act. Basically, entrepreneurship is the ability to create and build an enterprise or organization from scratch. The entrepreneur must be willing to take personal, and often financial, risks. He or she must find resources (both human and financial), assemble them for a purpose, and control them carefully. Most new enterprises are small businesses. Most small businesses require entrepreneurial skills on the part of the owners or managers.

There are approximately 15 million nonfarm businesses in the United States and Canada. Most of these enterprises are small. Almost anyone can start a business. Some entrepreneurs have been very successful. Others have failed. Those who fail can, and often do, try again. While it is easy to start a business it is relatively difficult to build a large new enterprise. Of the 15 million nonfarm businesses, fewer than four percent have sales of over one million dollars.

The successful entrepreneur requires many skills: creativity, ability to calculate risks, ability to minimize risks, ability to plan, and ability to work very hard. Almost anyone can try. Age is no barrier: Steve Jobs, creator of Apple Computers, was a millionaire before 30; Colonel Sanders launched his fried chicken business after his retirement at age 65.

The biggest problem facing the new business is survival. Approximately a half million new businesses are started up each year in the United States. Unfortunately, for every three new businesses that open in a year, two others close. Small firms, especially in retailing, construction, and services, show the highest rate of failure. By the end of the first year, 40 percent of all new businesses close their doors. After 10 years, 90 percent of all new businesses have closed. Failure may be a step in the learning process for many entrepreneurs.

There are countless approaches to establishing a new business, however, three elements are key to the process: the entrepreneurs, the business opportunity, and the resources needed for the enterprise. The entrepreneur needs skills and knowledge for the enterprise. Entrepreneurial drive and motivation to succeed are critical factors. Most important is perseverance. New business founders tend to start their enterprises in the same fields that they have been working in. Experience is often important to ensure success.

The business opportunity is also a key element. A good idea in itself is not enough. The idea must be researched to determine its feasibility: Is there a need for the product? Will customers buy it? At what price and quantity? The entrepreneur should prepare a business plan to help adequately research these questions.

Once the business opportunity has been assessed, the entrepreneur must seek the resources to start and operate the new enterprise. Use of a business plan is helpful if outside capital is required from a lender or equity participant. Before someone will lend or participate in founding a new enterprise they would like to see financial, marketing, and operating forecasts for the new venture.

Once a new enterprise has been started, it requires effective management if it is to succeed. The manager of a new business must know the market, the competition, the product, and the industry in general. Attracting, keeping, and motivating people are key skills for the entrepreneur. Knowledge of business finance and accounting is also helpful. Ability to analyze is important. Equally important is the ability to make a decision and carry it out.

A recent study by McKinsey & Company of growth companies shows that these companies achieved their successes initially with a unique product or a different way of doing business. Product quality and service to the customers were key elements.

Generally, the new enterprise, if successful, will go through a phase of high growth in the early years. At some point in time it will mature. The established, mature company may need very different managerial skills than those required in the start-up and rapid growth phase.

Many times, the new or small business is a family business. People sometimes make the mistake of assuming that because it is a family business, it is not necessary to spell out the specific responsibilities of each family member or financial commitment, including share of equity. Family bickering because these details were not spelled out in writing at the beginning has destroyed many businesses. The second or later generation family member who is considering joining a family business must assess whether the family business will meet his or her career goals better than another opportunity. Is the business large enough for more than one family member to have a useful and growing role? Can a son get on with his father? How long will the son have to wait to have real authority in the firm? Sometimes it is useful for the son or daughter to acquire experience at another company before joining the family business. This outside experience may help gain acceptance for the younger family member more quickly.

One way the potential entrepreneur can evaluate whether they are suited to entrepreneurship is the use of the *personal strategy assessment*. This assessment enables one to examine goals, aspirations, past performance, strengths, and weaknesses in order to better decide on a long-term personal strategy. As described in Jeffrey A. Timmons's *New Venture Creation*, (Second Edition, Richard D. Irwin, 1985), the personal strategy assessment is divided into four parts: self-assessing entrepreneurial roots; self-assessing entrepreneurial attributes and role requirements; goal setting and goal assessing; and partner, peer, and professional feedback.

Key to success in a new enterprise is planning. Plans often fail because realistic goals that can be measured in a specific period of time are not detailed. The entrepreneur must work with his management team to develop a plan with built-in performance goals spelled out. Plans should be reviewed periodically to take advantage of experience and feedback, however, plans should not be carved in stone. As experience in the new enterprise is gained, the plan must be revised. What is important is having long-term goals and a plan for getting there.

One of the key problems in small business is obtaining the resources (physical, monetary, and human) needed to carry out the goals of the new enterprise. Large organizations have access to many resources. The entrepreneur must make do with less. He or she must learn to "bootstrap" resources to achieve the goals of the enterprise. One way to bootstrap is to borrow resources from others — friends, relatives, suppliers, and customers can all lend credit or invest in the new firm. A garage, basement, or an in-home office can be a start for facilities. Use of a friend's copier or telephone line and even bartering can help a company begin its operation. A new enterprise can contract out portions of a project. For example, the firm may use an outside secretarial service to type proposals before cash flow permits hiring a full-time secretary. The new business can call on an accountant, an attorney, and specialized consultants for advice as needed without having an accountant or attorney or other specialist on full-time salary. Such specialists can be very helpful if used wisely. Help can also be obtained by selecting some experienced business people to serve on the board of directors of the new enterprise, often with minimal compensation.

Much information is available to the manager of a new enterprise. Many useful reference books are on shelves at local libraries. The Small Business Administration (SBA) can often supply useful advice. Personal computers and software for many applications are now readily available at moderate prices. Word processing on a personal computer may significantly reduce secretarial and clerical costs. Use of a spreadsheet for financial data can provide realism for planning. Software is available to help prepare payrolls and corporate income taxes.

One often hears, "Why put up with the uncertainties of running your own business?" "Stay with your job, and let the boss do the worrying." And it may be good advice for a lot of people who consider self-employment too hazardous, or for those with no aptitude for being proprietors or employers. With social security, retirement pensions, etc., many anticipate that continued employment is a fairly comfortable way of life. So why take a chance!

This is a controversial subject. Many people consider the advantages and disadvantages of working for someone else versus self-employment. Often a spouse may say, "I'm glad John has a steady job and does not have to worry about the business expense." Another spouse may say, "I wish Mary had a business of her own. With so many ahead of her for promotion, it will be hard for her to achieve success in a big company."

To many thousands each year there is but one answer. Perhaps impressed by the history of those who started out with little else but determination to carve out a future for themselves and who made America great in commerce and industry, they are not interested in looking forward to continued employment. To them, the phrases, "a land of opportunity" and "free enterprise" mean opportunity and freedom for them also to venture into the world of business, to succeed or not succeed according to their ability and effort, in competition with others.

Business is as old as humanity itself and just as commonplace. Everyone knows in a general way what business is, but many are dismayed to find how little they know of the way to operate a business with success. There is much to learn, and experience is the best teacher. Unfortunately, experience can sometimes be disheartening and expensive when one is not prepared.

Some things that have to be learned seem to be so simple they are frequently disregarded as unessential. Neglect of these basic principles or "rules" has caused many failures. When one engages in business with serious intent, he or she is participating in a complex activity where millions of men and women, all more or less linked together, are giving their best in daily thought and effort, all being maintained in harmonious relationship and in progressive movement by adherence to the "rules" of business.

To understand this better, one might reflect upon the question, "What is the general purpose of business?" The answer is: "The purpose of business is to serve some useful purpose." It must do something for somebody to justify its existence. As long as a business serves a useful purpose, there is a place for it in the business world. To the degree that it serves, it prospers.

Manufacturers study the need of the people, then undertake to design and produce what they think the people will buy to fulfill that need.

Wholesalers buy what the manufacturer produces, find retailers or dealers to buy from them, let the consumer know what is available, and make it convenient for the goods to be purchased. The manufacturer cannot continue to produce unless he or she knows that the wholesaler and retailer will continue to buy. Each business performs some service for the other business and for the consumer.

Since business consists of an endless variety of activities, the above illustration may not seem to apply to that which the reader has in mind. The underlying *principle* does apply, however, to each and every business and to all professions as well. When one is looking for an opportunity to start a business, or improve it, he or she searches for a locality where a need exists and plans then to supply it.

If wise, he or she will also carefully evaluate their own qualifications and improve them where necessary before starting. If this is neglected, the business may not last long. Some manage to continue in a state of half-dormant existence, derelicts on the sea of business, surviving somehow on the crumbs of patronage that happen to fall their way, and often just a nuisance to other businesses.

Proprietors who fall into careless habits of indifference toward customer goodwill need to have their eyes opened. Strange to say, they can often see the errors made in the management of another's place of business, but cannot see their own. They may complain about competition yet fail to exert themselves to do the things necessary to hold onto their customers.

To serve well as a merchant means to have a convenient, clean, and attractive place to receive customers; neat, courteous, and competent employees; fresh and complete stocks attractively displayed; prices always in line; and an atmosphere that is always reminding the customers that their patronage is welcome and appreciated.

The United States Chamber of Commerce has outlined the following as a suggested maxim for business generally:

1. *For Customers:* That they may have the best at lowest cost consistent with fairness to all engaged in production and distribution.

2. *For Workers:* That their welfare will not be sacrificed for the benefit of others; that in their employment relations, their rights will be respected.

3. *For Management:* That it may be recognized in proportion to its demonstrated ability, considering always the proper interest of others.

4. *For Competitors:* That there will be avoidance of every form of unfair competition.

5. *For Investors:* That their rights will be safeguarded and that they will be kept informed so that they can exercise their own judgment respecting their interests.

6. *For the Public:* That the business will strive in all its operations and relations to promote the general welfare and, without yielding its rights of petition and protest, to observe faithfully the laws of the land.

2
Qualifications of a Proprietor

Operating a small business or a new enterprise is not the prerogative of any particular kind of people of any age or sex. Nor can proprietors be classified as those possessing certain qualifications of academic education, intelligence, or personality. Various people have started or are thinking of starting a small business of their own. Excessive funds can be a hindrance, and those with the smallest resources often score the best. Some cannot be content to be employed by others in any permanent position. They must captain their own ship, direct their own business destiny, and seriously plan to operate a business as a career.

The desire, or necessity, to work for pocket money in one's youth for schooling expense, or to help family finances, has given many an insight into business. This kind of experience builds self-confidence and develops an understanding of basic business principles, often saving years of trial and error later on. If he or she continues, one learns how to handle money, relationships with customers, business possibilities, and responsibilities.

When a person looks upon a business venture as an opportunity for personal achievement and welcomes the responsibilities which business brings, he or she is well on the road to success. On the other hand, if one has the mistaken idea that owning his or her own business is an escape from the direction and possible criticism of a boss, he or she is in for a big disappointment. Business, in itself, is a strict disciplinarian and the proprietor may not like many things the business requires to be done.

Some individuals have the idea to buy a going business about which they know little. They think it will go along automatically, producing an income without undue exertion. Owning a business is not that simple. It is more like buying a job with the tools for doing the job. It is up to the purchaser to furnish the knowledge, experience, and effort. For instance, a man experienced in the business of dairy farming may buy a cow that he knows is a good producer of milk. He estimates that such a purchase will enable him to sell several gallons of milk each month at a profit. He also knows it is his responsibility to take care of the cow, to provide pasture, feed, and labor, and to find customers to buy the milk.

The cow would probably become discouraged very quickly and stop giving milk if the farmer did not do his part. So it would be also with a business if the new owner did not know how to run it and did not do what was necessary to keep it producing.

When an individual acquires a business, the new proprietor has the privilege of directing its operation. The proprietor should also take on the obligations of managing it conscientiously, with the same attitude he or she would have if employed to do so by some other owner. A good procedure to remind the proprietor that compensation must be earned is to take a regular salary as manager. Then, of course, he or she does as they wish with any profit the business may make for any period.

Even though ownership and management are vested in the same person, it is good practice to consider the business as entirely separate from the owner's personal affairs. This is not a simple or easy thing to do. With any small business, it is difficult to separate the proprietor's rights and responsibilities from those of the business, particularly in money matters.

A business is not concerned with its owner's personal debts or obligations except where they apply directly to the business. Apart from providing wages or salaries, it is not the function of the business to pay living expenses, payments on a home, for a family member's surgery, or for support of relatives not employed in the business — that is, not with the money needed by the business to meet its obligations. If and when there is a profit, that money may be used by the proprietor for whatever personal use chosen.

Having the responsibility of managing the daily operation of a business, the owner cannot neglect it by taking time out to play golf or go fishing.

Like the farmer who was not interested in more efficient methods of farming because he said he knew of lots better ways already but was not using them, there are proprietors of other businesses who insist on following their own whims and fancies rather than taking the trouble to learn and use good business procedure. It is not strange that they are generally the ones who are always complaining about business being bad, there being too much competition, and other troubles.

Good business practices are sought after and put into use when the proprietor looks upon the business as a valuable producing property, entitled to the best personal service he or she can give it. The proprietor takes pride in the opportunity and makes every effort to use good judgment in its operation.

Many have learned the hard way, starting with no preparation, dependent entirely on what they might learn from trial and error. Some have eventually become successful. A relative few have become famous through their careers from "rags to riches." Unfortunately, a much larger percentage have failed through their lack of ability to cope with business problems.

Many have been successful due to the knowledge and skill acquired while being employed by others, using this ability as a basis to start their own business. If others have failed, perhaps it is because they were unable to see the difference between being an employee and being their own boss or employer.

There is a distinct difference, not only as to position, but in one's mental attitude toward the business and toward everyone and everything connected with it. The position of boss carries with it many responsibilities. Only those employees who have had some experience in carrying these responsibilities — perhaps as a manager or superintendent — can readily understand this.

Many employees are inclined to believe there is nothing much to learn about managing a business; that if one is competent to do some specific thing pertaining to a business in serving its customers, everything else is relatively unimportant and quickly learned.

The trained and skilled automobile mechanic, who may be tops in his special field, may have the idea that he now knows and does just about everything of importance to the business while the boss just sits at his desk taking in money and signing checks.

A star salesman may regard his or her ability to bring in orders as the only really necessary qualification for running a business. Many individuals with fine records as salesmen fail when they try it alone without the guiding hand of a boss.

A pharmacist, employed exclusively in the prescription department of a large drug store, may aspire to run her own drugstore. It takes years of study to become a registered pharmacist, and the work of filling prescriptions is unquestionably very important. But if she continues to do nothing else but fill prescriptions, and that is the sum total of her business knowledge and experience, she may never qualify to manage a drug store. While prescription work is the basic requirement, it plays a minor role in the successful operation of a modern drug store.

To obtain the broader experience of buying and selling general merchandise, food, drinks, candy, and smoking supplies, the ambitious pharmacist may have to quit her job and find employment in a smaller store as a general clerk or assistant manager in order to learn something about the other elements of the business.

Some employers may give employees the privilege of transferring from one department to another in order to gain all-around experience. Ambition is generally recognized, appreciated, and rewarded by employers, but businesses are not operated as "prep" schools for young people who are ambitious to run their own businesses.

Many employees lack the ability to supervise others. When given an assistant or put in charge of a group, they do not seem to have the "knack" of getting along well with those whom they are assigned to direct. They may be unable to plan the work efficiently or they may fail to inspire teamwork. They may assume an attitude that is too "bossy" and be resented by those placed under them.

A competent waitress may be a failure as a dining room supervisor because she has not had the opportunity, or possibly the desire, to develop her managing ability. Until she does, she is not ready to run her own restaurant.

The skilled mechanic, efficient in his own work, may be a poor foreman or superintendent because he has not yet learned that planning the work and directing others is just as important to the business as is his own skill.

A strictly "one-person" business does not get very far in the commercial world. If one now employed is looking forward to operating his or her own business, he or she should analyze their own personal qualifications for supervising others. Some may be naturally gifted in this respect. Others may have to study and practice in order to acquire proficiency in training, directing, and inspiring their co-workers if they are to be successful employers.

Obviously, it is desirable to have experience in all phases of business operation. Where there is a known lack, it may be good judgment to postpone starting the business until such time as the necessary experience is acquired.

In any field of business, one of the greatest compliments a businessperson can receive is to have people say, "That person knows their business." When customers pass that word along, the "person who knows his or her business" is receiving priceless advertising and will probably get all the business that can be handled.

The business world answers the question, "What experience is necessary to operate a business?" by saying: "It must be sufficient to enable the proprietor to render a service to the buying public that is superior, or at least comparable, to that of his or her competitors."

To be capable of surviving competition, which every businessperson may well expect to have, means capability in management, knowledge and experience in bookkeeping, purchasing, selling, advertising, and financing; all of which may be supplementary to the technicalities of any particular business.

3
The Art of
Handling Money

The businessperson's attitude toward money used in a business is quite different from his or her attitude toward personal funds. Business money takes on somewhat the nature of a commodity, like merchandise or stock, and is considered as a working tool for business. Therefore, it loses some of its glamour but takes on a new importance.

The newcomer in the business world may not see the difference and argue that money in the cash register and cash in a pocket are one and the same thing. There must be a definite distinction made between the two. One serves a business purpose and is managed accordingly; the other serves a personal purpose in which business is not interested.

The proprietor may be careless or indifferent about *personal* finances — that is his or her privilege — but not so with the funds used in the business. Good business management does not permit any trifling or inefficiency in the handling of this important tool of business. Every business penny must be kept under strict control and accounted for at all times. Every business dollar must be a hard-working dollar.

Those who have learned something of the art of handling money, by practicing economy and good judgment in the spending of their personal funds, have something valuable in this experience that will be a great help to them in running their own business. Those who have not practiced economy in their spending have a difficult lesson to learn.

At the very beginning, before the business is in actual operation, the money that is to be put into the business should be regarded as distinctly separate funds from other money that the proprietor has for personal use. As the business is being organized, the proprietor will want to segregate what is spent on the business from what is spent for personal needs.

The correct procedure is to start with the business money deposited in the bank in a separate account, drawing checks against this account for business expenditures. This starts the business off in a businesslike way, protecting the money against loss and tracking what is spent. Minor expenditures for small cash purchases are provided for by drawing and cashing a check in advance, a record of which is made on the check stub. This should be sufficient to cover minor expenses.

If the cash funds are not segregated and small purchases are made carelessly, with haphazard accounting for these expenditures, it is the beginning of a bad habit that hinders the success of many small businesses.

Money in business is never undervaluated. Every penny is considered important and all cash on hand is carefully guarded and accounted for. It is protected by keeping it in a locked cash drawer, cash register, or safe, carefully counted and checked against daily cash expenditures.

Some may feel that this care borders on penuriousness and, as employees, may be apt to ridicule the proprietor for taking such pains to count every penny in the cash drawer so frequently. However, as they become more experienced in business, they learn that this is not being close-fisted or stingy. It is a very necessary procedure and conforms to good business practice.

Access to cash should always be closely restricted, generally to one person, who is held responsible. Many proprietors of small businesses have difficulty keeping their cash straight, particularly if more than one person is permitted access to the cash.

The proprietor is often the offender, particularly if he or she holds to the idea that the cash in the drawer belongs to him or her as the proprietor and he or she is privileged to do with it as he or she pleases. Perhaps that is the proprietor's own affair, but so is the matter of running a business in a businesslike way. If a person chooses to follow whims rather than confirmed good business practices, he or she may someday wake up to the fact that the business amounts to very little.

As the business grows, a cashier may be employed for the specific purpose of taking care of the business cash on hand. This is a recognized vocation, and both proprietors and cashiers have learned by experience that there is just one way to run this job. The practice used by proprietors and cashiers in nearly every line of business is to maintain a separate cashier's fund, or "bank," consisting of various denominations of currency to facilitate making change. A separate locked box or cash drawer is provided for the cashier's use and the fund is handed to the cashier when he or she comes on duty.

A good businessperson never takes any liberties with the money in the cashier's fund while it is in the custody of the cashier. That would be unfair to the one who is being held responsible. A good cashier will insist that no one else touches this money. Experience has taught that the best way for everyone to keep out of trouble, to avoid suspicious and unpleasant happenings, is to treat this volatile commodity of business with the respect that it deserves.

Money is a valuable working tool or medium. The proprietor uses money to buy what can be resold at a profit, as a revolving fund to replenish depleted stocks, to carry customers' charge accounts, and to pay operating expenses, etc. Money wisely invested is far more valuable than money lying idle.

Handling money used in a business is like handling money belonging to a friend. It carries a different and greater responsibility than personal spending.

4

Purchasing

"Whatever is sold must first be bought!"

Buy and sell. Buy and sell again. Buy and sell again and again is the constant revolving cycle of business and generally its main function in handling all commodities, from peanuts to real estate.

That which is bought wisely can be sold at a profit. That which is not bought wisely must eventually be sold at a loss.

Knowledge of *purchasing* and ability to buy wisely are very necessary qualifications for everyone running his or her own business. This knowledge is acquired only through careful study and experience.

The inexperienced businessperson must learn how to buy the particular commodity in which he or she proposes to deal, how to arrive at the right price for that commodity, from whom it is best to buy, and at what terms. Still more important, the buyer must carefully determine how and when he or she is going to sell the purchased commodity before it is actually bought.

Business never fails to penalize poor judgment or carelessness in purchasing, but always rewards good judgment.

Employees rarely have the opportunity to acquire enough experience in this important element of business. Generally, it is the well-guarded privilege of the "boss," whose money must pay for the purchases.

Some knowledge of purchasing may be picked up by observation and asking a lot of questions or by seeking competent advice, particularly on initial or unusual purchases. A study of available market prices, procuring and comparing competitive bids, and keeping an eye open for good buys that may be available are also helpful.

Such opportunities can occur any day in business, and the clever businessperson is quick to grasp the chance to make an added profit.

Generally, there is competition between suppliers. This helps to establish a fair price on most commodities. Much can be learned by comparing and averaging several quotations from different suppliers offering similar goods or articles.

Consideration should also be given to discounts and terms allowed, quantities necessary to buy to get better price, delivery or transportation charges, and other services, such as return or replacement privileges that the supplier may offer.

"Whatever is bought in business must eventually be sold!" But to be compelled to sell anything *eventually* is not a pleasing thought to any businessperson. He does not buy to sell *eventually*. He or she buys to sell quickly, *and at a profit*. Therefore, the businessperson pauses before committing in order to ask some questions:

- ■ Is the quality acceptable?
- ■ What are the quick sales possibilities of this purchase?
- ■ What margin of profit can I expect to make?
- ■ Is the quantity offered the right quantity, conforming to quick sales possibilities, or will a large part of it become slow-moving overstocks, gathering dust on the shelves and tying up much needed capital?

Suppliers are generally interested in volume selling, offering premiums in lower cost, extra discounts, bonuses, special services, or other inducements for a quantity order. Sometimes, such propositions are very interesting and worthwhile, but unless the buyer is certain of disposing of the goods to complete satisfaction, it is much smarter to take the smaller quantity even though the potential profit is less. Profit on many sales is often wiped out by having to dispose of overstocks at a loss. One bad purchase can offset several good purchases.

Signing an order is a definite commitment or contract to buy. The seller expects, and may legally compel, the buyer to accept and pay for what he or she orders, unless a cancellation privilege is incorporated into the order or contract.

Buying for remote future delivery, or contracting to buy certain quantities over a long period of time, is hazardous business. Time is an all-important factor in business. Over the course of time, styles change, new models and products are made available, and consumer buying habits and business conditions may change. Some or all of these may make a proprietor wish he or she had not agreed to buy the items.

Figuratively speaking, "Always have the goods sold before you buy" is a good rule to follow.

On the other hand, the businessperson may wish to speculate on some commodity. Speculation may be the business. One entrepreneur may buy quantities that appear tremendous to another. Sometimes it is just a gamble, but it may be that the buyer of large quantities has ample confidence in the purchase and in the ability to sell advantageously when the appropriate time comes.

Business may be a gamble to some, but most businesspeople do not look upon business that way. They do not gamble on the "chance" of obtaining money somehow to pay for their purchases. Generally, they have good and ample reason to believe they will have funds on hand to meet their obligations as they become due, and are not obliged to "rob Peter to pay Paul."

When buying office or business furniture, accessories, and equipment, the best of judgment must be used. Such things are generally necessary to the business, but the questions should be: How necessary? What is each article contributing to the profit-making capacity of the business? If they do not materially contribute, such purchases may turn out to be expensive luxuries, tying up capital needed for productive purposes.

The farmer each year stakes the cost of seed, fertilizer, and labor against the possibility of a paying crop to be harvested many months later. If nature treats him kindly with sunshine, rain, no damaging droughts, floods, or high winds, and when he sells his crop the market price is sufficiently high to give him a profit over his costs, the operation of his business of farming has been successful for that year.

All businesses are a gamble, more or less, but the successful farmer or businessperson is never a gambler in the sense that they speculate purely on chance. The entrepreneur buys to sell or produce at a profit and feels convinced by a study of the market that he or she can sell at profit before buying or producing the commodity(ies).

Among entrepreneurs, are all degrees of human temperaments — from the timid, ultra-conservative to the rashly speculative. The timid and too conservative never quite qualify for the title *"A Progressive Businessperson."* Timidity has no place in business. On the other hand, the incurable speculator may have a few flashy successes, but too often winds up poorer than when he or she started.

Obviously, the middle course is the right one. Business owners must be ever on the alert to see and grasp the special opportunities for buying what can be resold at a profit. Otherwise, the bargains are grabbed by those who are more wide awake. However, one must be able to resist the highly speculative ventures that appear to be enticingly profitable. Successful businesses are built on a foundation of good business judgment as a base for progressive policies of operation.

While there is an endless variety in the kinds of businesses, routine buying and selling is much more common than speculation in the operation of most businesses.

5
Selling

To sell any product, material, or service to another for money or its equivalent is to participate in a business transaction. Operating a business — any business — is simply engaging in a series or multiplicity of transactions, and every transaction constitutes a sale made to someone.

SELLING IS THE SUSTAINING AND
MOTIVATING ELEMENT OF ALL BUSINESSES

This includes doctors or other professional people who must continue to sell their services either directly or indirectly if they are to continue their practice. Therefore, no experienced businessperson underestimates the importance of learning all he or she can about the great art of selling.

Some proprietors of small businesses profess to know nothing about selling, and many businesses are operated without the services of those who are specifically classified as salespersons. However, these businesses are all making sales. Therefore, it is obvious that someone, probably the proprietor, is selling.

It is not always necessary to have specific training and experience as a salesperson, but it is necessary to realize the importance of selling and apply good sales practices to every detail of business operation.

Selling is not the exclusive function of clerks standing behind a counter, or salespeople calling on customers with catalog and order book in hand. It is the function of everyone connected with every business who can do anything that may make customers *want to buy*. This can encompass any employee from the porter who keeps the premises clean to the delivery person transporting and delivering goods.

Selling begins with setting up the business and buying or making available the goods or services that prospective customers may need or want. It means giving the customers the opportunity to purchase, letting them know what is available, and making it interesting for customers to buy.

There are always people somewhere who will have use for whatever is offered for sale. It is the purpose of business and the business owner to find these customers and generate the sales.

Good selling practice includes, in some cases, the study and analysis of the customers' needs. It may include demonstration and instruction. It may include helping the customer decide what and when they will buy. This does not mean talking loud and fast, literally hypnotizing the customer into buying. Such selling practice is not condoned generally by the business world, which has a huge and serious job in supplying the real needs of the people.

There exists plenty of "high-pressure" selling, not between the retail dealer and customers, but between manufacturers and wholesalers and the retail dealers. Some of these wholesale suppliers claim it is necessary to "high-pressure" the dealer to keep him or her from falling asleep on the selling job. Unfortunately, this *is* true with many proprietors of small businesses. They are likely to lapse into lethargy in their sales effort and rely too heavily on the possibility of customers buying anyway, whether they do their part or not.

The merchant who expects to hold a place for his or her business in the business world and in the minds of customers assumes obligations that must be fulfilled. The merchant will not be very successful if the quality of goods is questionable, or if prices are out of line with the market, or if his or her sales effort is lax.

If the retailer obtains the right cost price to enable selling at a profit and is given the opportunity to sell a line of merchandise with a popular appeal to the consumer, the manufacturer or wholesaler has the right to expect the retailer to exert himself to make sales. Otherwise, the manufacturer is deprived of the potential sales for the product in the community where the merchant is located. The customers who may want to buy such goods or articles are also entitled to the opportunity to buy them.

The idle dream of the indolent proprietor is to have a market all to himself or herself, where sales just roll in without any selling effort on his or her part. Fortunately for everyone, competition is usually at hand to force business owners to exert themselves, and to fight for the sales they do get.

The weapon that successful businesspersons use is *salesmanship,* aggressively used in all its broad phases and in every detail of the operation of their businesses. *Salesmanship* in itself is an interesting study. One always finds something here that is applicable to everyday business in every kind of organization.

Some of the principles of *salesmanship* apply to employees as well as to proprietors. These principles teach the value of personality, personal neatness, courtesy, and orderliness in business, as well as a host of other tangible and intangible elements essential to business progress. *Salesmanship* can help the office boy to get a better job, or it may be vital to the successful culmination of a million-dollar deal.

Whole libraries of books and many courses of instruction are available on the teaching of salesmanship. The objective here is not to attempt to cover the subject, but to encourage the proprietor of a small business to study this important function as it applies to the particular business owned.

.

6
Advertising

Advertising is anything and everything the proprietor may do to let prospective customers know the name and address of the business and what the business offers for sale. Everything that helps to build up the business is good advertising. Whatever is done that hurts the business is bad advertising. Everything that the customer sees, hears, or knows about the business is some form of advertising, either good or bad.

Advertising — the good kind — is the working tool for making sales. Its only purposes are to sell, to bring in new customers, and to hold old customers. Some businesspeople, in their zeal to attract new customers, forget about taking care of their old ones. They spend a lot of money trying to capture new customers without ensuring they are doing the things necessary to hold existing loyal customers whose patronage they had already earned. This just does not make sense, but it is happening every day.

Hundreds of millions of dollars are spent each year in the nationwide effort to sell what the country produces. Advertising is a tremendous force in business and a highly developed and complex business in itself. It is a big and comprehensive study in its various forms of radio, television, national magazine and newspaper advertising, trade papers, direct mail, house organs, and road signs, among others.

No proprietor of a small business is expected to be an expert on this subject unless advertising happens to *be* his business. But every business must let its customers know what it is and where the business is located, and what it has to sell. Therefore, the business must do some form(s) of advertising. The proprietor cannot afford to contract an expert for advice unless an extensive advertising program is planned, so the small business must learn to plan its own advertising the best it can.

It is here, as in so many phases of business, that one can learn a great deal by observation and study of what others are doing. Careful study of what is bringing success to others will point the way. It is common and good practice in business to do as successful business leaders do. Originality always has its place and possible value, but it is no sin in business to copy successes. To the contrary, it is very good business practice to observe and learn everything possible that is helping another person's business and adapt it to one's own organization.

Every detail of the business "front" to the customer must be carefully scrutinized and carefully improved as necessary, with the idea of creating a favorable impression on customers. Advertising includes the outdoor signs and appearance of the business premises, the attractiveness, cleanliness, and orderliness of the interior; the freshness and quality of merchandise offered; the appearance and mannerisms of both employees and the proprietor; and promptness, reliability, and every other element of service. Every sale made carries with it some advertising.

The advertising of a new, small business may be simply by "word of mouth," where one customer tells another if favorably impressed. It may be by printed business card, painted sign, or small advertisement in the local paper. These may appear to be very simple things, but they are vitally important to a new, small business. It is a "first-grade" lesson in the art of advertising and, as such, every detail is worthy of careful study and planning.

There will be need for further study on this subject as the business progresses. Advertising is continuously essential to business. One must eventually become adept in planning, and then in obtaining, expert advice in the use of this important activity for business success and growth. Advertising is too valuable a working tool for selling to be handled carelessly or without any knowledge and skill.

7

Progressiveness

Progressiveness is the vital spark, the dynamic force, and the continuing motive power that vitalizes a business, keeps pushing it along, makes it grow, and eventually enables it to occupy the position of a solid establishment in the business world.

Progressiveness emanates from the directing mind of the business — usually the proprietor. Not all persons have this qualification. Some have it spasmodically, unable to keep it continuously sustained to a point of effectiveness.

To be progressive in business means many things. It begins with the proprietor being a vigorous manager, eager to make headway with the chosen work and willing to put in long hours if necessary. It includes the desire to improve the owner's knowledge of things essential to the success of the business, to search for, find, and put into use new ideas in advertising, displaying, and selling, new ideas for better methods pertaining to any element of the business, or new services that appeal to customers.

The progressive business owner is always on the alert to pick up helpful information. He or she scans the trade periodicals and newspapers to keep abreast of the times on all things pertaining to the business. The owner studies the advertising and technique of competitors.

The owner takes particular pains to avoid getting "into a rut" and arranges periodically to get "outside" the business in order to get a fresh perspective. The proprietor acquires the habit of "seeing" the business through the eyes of the customers, critically scrutinizing all details of his or her own service. The owner takes an active part in his trade association, Chamber of Commerce, and civic gatherings, learning much from contacts with other business owners.

The place of business is sparkling clean, well-ordered, and in good taste. Merchandise is clean, neatly arranged, and attractively displayed. Employees are courteous and competent. The owner's desk is kept in order, not littered with accumulations of old papers and junk. Business correspondence is always kept smartly up to the minute.

In all, a well-organized business is like a complete and perfectly regulated machine, ready and capable of full production as the motivating power of progressiveness is applied.

These are some of the things that tell the world whether a business owner is progressive or not.

Almost every new business is fairly progressive at the start, energized by the enthusiasm of the proprietor in the new venture. This enthusiasm must not be permitted to lag. The business will always need this motivation, as each day brings new opportunities for the exercise of progressiveness. Business does not live on the accomplishments of yesterday. It is always preparing for the bigger and better accomplishments of tomorrow.

A farmer, when refusing to subscribe to a magazine which featured modern, progressive methods in farming, said to the student solicitor: "Son, why should I learn more about farming when I ain't farming half as good now as I know how?"

And so it is with some proprietors of small businesses. Somewhere back they lost their enthusiasm and are now content to carry on their business about "half as good as they know how." The spirit of progressiveness just "kinda wilted" and died. Perhaps it was none too robust to begin with, not strong enough to compete for the proprietor's attention when the "alibis" came drifting his way.

"Business is terrible." "Can't get the capital to work with." "Can't collect what people owe me." When a person's mind is chock full of alibis, there is no room for the spirit of progressiveness to squeeze in.

When a person tires of his or her business and it becomes drudgery, far better for the owner to close it out promptly than to continue in a half-hearted manner. The owner's time can probably be spent to better advantage if employed by someone else, and neither his customers nor the business world will miss him.

There is no danger, generally, of being too progressive, but over-optimism is sometimes confused with progressiveness. This is particularly true in the case when planning business expansion. For instance, a business may be thriving in quarters that are so cramped and crowded that the proprietor feels the necessity of moving or enlarging the place of business. Plans are made to provide better and more modern equipment and facilities for the growing business, thus permitting customers more comfort and convenience.

There can be no doubt regarding the proprietor's ability to operate or to his or her progressiveness. But in plans for the larger place, there must be a good deal of conservatism to balance the optimism, together with careful calculations of the probable increased sales, operation costs, and capital charges. The non-progressives do not have this problem, since their businesses seldom need larger quarters, but it is a critical matter to move any business, particularly one that is going strong in a place that may be considered too small.

Customers have the peculiarity of wanting to go where the crowds go, and even if the location will hold only a very small "crowd," it appears to be very busy and, therefore, *must* be a good place to deal. If the proprietor makes the mistake of having the new place too big, or if it appears to be too elaborate and high-priced, it may lose money faster than the smaller place could make it.

The owner may lose a lot of his old customers who have become accustomed to dealing in the small store. They may resent the appearance of the proprietor as being too prosperous in the beautiful new place. Should all the old customers be retained, they may still be too few for the larger establishment.

Many progressive business owners have the fault of over-optimism and try to make in one jump what should take two. They may build their organization and facilities too fast for the possible increase in their customer trade and suffer the trials of over-expansion. Being hustlers, however, and not easily discouraged, they can resolve these difficulties in time.

8
Business Ethics

In business, as well as in the professions, there are unwritten rules of conduct or behavior which are generally accepted and more or less lived up to as a sort of business Golden Rule.

For instance, a successful businessperson does not make derogatory remarks about competitors' services or merchandise. The proprietor may point out to the customer why one thinks one's service or product is better, supporting such claims with demonstration and proof. But the owner is careful to avoid running down the competitor's product or business, or offending in other ways. A general assertion may be that the competitor's product is unquestionably good, but "our product is better and we will be happy to prove it."

The entrepreneur may advertise that the business gives the best bargains in the city and handles the finest merchandise, but does not say his competitor handles cheap and inferior merchandise, or overcharges for what is sold.

The owner may be consistently aggressive in competing for business. Through smart buying, the owner may be in a position to offer superior merchandise at lower prices. He or she may be able to keep competitors guessing as to what will be done next to appeal to the public for their patronage, but whatever the owner does must be "clean" competition and above reproach. The owner does not resort to trickery, or making petty concessions in price or service to entice a customer away from a competitor.

A smart businessperson does not indulge in "cutthroat" price wars and has learned the fallacy of such practices, knowing that, in the end, the aggressor frequently gets the worst of it.

Another problem in ethics concerns pirating employees away from other firms. When the applicant is hired, the proprietor should insist that the applicant's employer be given proper notice and time to engage a substitute before the new employee is permitted to start work on the new job. Business owners should try to do unto other employers as they would have done unto them. Hence, an owner should feel free to inquire of the other employer about the new employee's honesty or other qualifications. Employers generally maintain this mutual privilege and benefit.

Keeping appointments promptly, on the minute, is a business obligation and a courtesy that is always appreciated. Busy persons must schedule their time in order to accomplish the many things demanding their attention each working day. It is always presumed that appointments are made to conserve time, a commodity valuable to both parties. Failure to be prompt is sure to be disappointing, and an hour lost may throw the entire day off schedule for one or the other. If one is to be unavoidably delayed, a message to that effect should always be sent to the other party.

Salespersons calling on business owners are frequently imposed upon by being kept waiting while the proprietor gives time to less important matters. The salesperson cannot protest because he or she is anxious to have the good will of the proprietor. Business owners who also have persons out selling for them realize the cost of such wasted time and endeavor to give salespersons their attention as promptly as possible.

Answering business correspondence, at least acknowledging receipt by next return mail, is a business courtesy about which no business owner can afford to be careless. The number of letters that remain unanswered for days and weeks is legion, and proprietors of small businesses are the worst offenders. The chaotic accumulation of new and old correspondence, catalogs, trade papers, samples, and junk on the proprietor's desk in back of the store is frequently an unholy sight to behold! Such carelessness is one of those costly things in which many small businesses indulge. "Big" business cannot afford such carelessness.

Keeping promises of all kinds — on deliveries, on starting a job or completing it — is more than a business courtesy. It is the fulfillment of an obligation that any good businessperson knows is a basic principle of business. Carelessness in making the promise is generally the cause of failure in keeping it. Some proprietors would be surprised to learn how much time is wasted in apologizing to and pacifying customers because of unfulfilled promises. Needless to say, customers invariably have long memories when they are disappointed. They take their patronage elsewhere next time.

Telephone courtesy may be considered a matter of business ethics, or just common sense. The tremendous amount of business done by telephone has made telephone salesmanship an art well worth cultivating. The phrase coined by a Bell Telephone company, "The voice with a smile wins," exemplifies the importance of telephone courtesy. *"Selling by Telephone"* is the title of one of this company's booklets and is familiar to many businesspersons.

The ethical businessperson does not indulge in ambiguous or misleading advertising, nor does he or she "high-pressure" customers to buy substitutes. The owner does not misrepresent in any way, but marks merchandise plainly and sells it for what it is. In short, he or she is upright and honest in all business dealings.

Is honesty the best policy? Some beginners are prone to say this old platitude is all "bunk!" Somewhere, somehow, they have picked up the idea that one must strive to get the best of the other fellow to be successful in business. Perhaps it emanates from ancient traders', *"Caveat emptor,"* "Let the buyer beware," or "He who buys needs a hundred eyes, he who sells but one." These old sayings and such principles have no part in modern successful business. Neither is there any room today for the "smart" salesperson, whose smartness consists of the ability to sell what the customer neither wants nor needs.

Honesty in business is now universally accepted as the only policy upon which any business can hope to survive. Full value at prices asked is generally the rule, not the exception, and one does not hesitate today to pay in advance for fear the merchant will fail to deliver the purchase. Of course, there are some merchants, as there are some customers, whose integrity is open to question, but the more and larger the business, the more scrupulously honest its policy. It cannot afford to be otherwise.

9
Aids for the Business Owner – Personal and Professional Services

As aids to business, the attorney, the auditor, and the banker are valuable business acquaintances to have. The friendly advice and assistance that these individuals can give, due to their specialized knowledge, will be of great help in the development of the business.

It is the function of individuals in these three classifications primarily to serve business, to interpret the law for business owners, to assist in keeping records of value to business owners, and to assist business owners in the financing of business transactions. The attorney, the auditor, and the banker take such an active and important part in the business world that all commerce and industry would come to an abrupt stop if their services were to be denied.

Many make the mistake by waiting until there is an urgent need before establishing such connections, whereas if these personal contacts are made available for friendly conference on business problems, emergencies may often be prevented.

The local *attorney* will be called on very early in the life of the business. The attorney's services will be of value in checking the first agreements or contracts entered into, or in the negotiation of a loan, or in organizing the business as a partnership or a corporation.

As the business progresses, there will be a multiplicity of legal questions coming up from time to time, where the business owner needs friendly and helpful guidance. An early acquaintanceship may develop into a highly valued business connection.

The local *auditor* or accountant is the expert on business records. The accountant's services are desirable in first selecting the simplest and best bookkeeping system for the business and for instruction in making the first entries. Thereafter, at monthly or other regular intervals, the accountant assists in getting, from the accumulated records of the period, the information that is essential for the proprietor to intelligently and efficiently run the business.

If the auditor is employed to analyze the books at frequent intervals, he or she becomes familiar with various elements of sales, costs, profits, and losses, and, through aptitude in analyzing, may be able to detect errors in operation that may not be apparent to the proprietor. This may be the only person, other than the owner, who has access to the confidential figures and with whom the owner may discuss confidential matters.

There are times when the "boss" needs someone to check up on him or her and there is no one more qualified than the friendly and competent auditor.

The local *banker is* a good person to have at least as a friendly acquaintance. Banks are continually receiving inquiries regarding the business reputation or standing of persons in their community. It would not be complimentary to a new business for the banker to have to say he or she didn't know of its existence.

Merchants would have a hard time getting along without the service of a local bank — to serve as a safe depository for the capital funds, to accept the daily receipts of cash and checks, to supply currency and small change, to provide a simple and safe means of paying bills by bank check, and to provide a monthly statement of checks and balances, which is a valuable auxiliary record of the cash account.

Such service is costly to the bank and generally there is a small monthly charge made for it, particularly if the bank balance is small. The principal revenue of banks, however, is not in charging depositors for taking care of their money. It is from interest earned on loans made to business. If the bank is able to make substantial loans to business at good interest rates, it is probably doing a profitable business and may waive its charges to depositors.

When approaching a banker for a business loan, the proper attitude is definitely not that of asking a personal favor; in fact, one very seldom asks personal favors of any kind in business. A loan, like any other business transaction, is affected by the interchange of equivalent values. One "hires" the use of money as one hires the use of a truck or a building.

Other personal services, professional and otherwise, are available to business owners when required. For instance, the *insurance agent* has a wealth of specialized knowledge of the needs of business owners for insurance protection. An *advertising agency* might assist in planning an advertising program.

The *wholesaler* is generally in a position to be of great help to retail dealers through his or her knowledge of trade conditions and other dealers' experience. Wholesalers know the specific items that go into making up a good stock of merchandise for the dealer, the new or fast sellers, and those that do not sell. Very often, the wholesaler will extend goodwill service to include valuable and conscientiously given advice to the new proprietor. Frequently, wholesalers will help dealers find items the wholesaler does not handle.

It is the wholesaler's function, of course, to sell what is profitable to sell, and in some cases, there may be some risk involved when the retailer is overloaded with merchandise that cannot be easily disposed. It is the buyer's responsibility to see that this does not happen.

The *trade papers* are one of the valued aids to business, and serve in nearly all fields of business activity. There is scarcely a business house anywhere that does not subscribe to one or more favorite trade publications.

The trade paper is one of the best means that business owners have of keeping themselves posted on what is new in merchandise or specialties and where they can be obtained. Here the manufacturer, the wholesaler, and supplier to the trade tell their story to the dealer.

Trade papers also make valuable contributions to business through their printed articles on various subjects of particular interest to business owners in that category of business, describing merchandising displays, advertising of various kinds, new selling ideas, office and record keeping systems, technical and servicing procedures.

Many business owners find it difficult to find time to read and absorb all the good suggestions to be found in trade papers, but generally agree on the value of such information.

10

On Being a Good Boss

Some are fortunate in being gifted with qualities for leading and directing others. They just naturally make good "bosses." Some will learn to acquire these qualities. Others will never learn because they cannot see that the position of boss entails responsibility as well as privilege.

Perhaps the foremost qualification for being a good boss lies in being *deserving of the respect of employees*. When the "boss" is respected, not alone for his or her position as employer but also for the boss's qualifications for leadership, all questions pertaining to the relationship between employer and employee are easily settled.

People do not succeed in business just because they have the means to purchase the material requisites of a business or pay salaries to others to work for them. Modern business places heavy demands on executives. They must have real ability to cope with complex business problems. No man or woman can hope to hold an important executive position in industry unless he or she can inspire others with sound and progressive leadership.

A good "boss" primarily is one who has complete mastery over all elements of the business and has the respect of the employees because they know the boss knows the business and can intelligently direct them. Add to that personal character above reproach, unquestioned fair and square dealing, outstanding courtesy, economy, and efficiency in business, and you have a pretty good "boss."

"Do as I say and not as I do" may suffice to get some things done while the employee is being watched, but if one has to spend time watching an employee, what is gained by employing him or her?

Perhaps when the boss's eyes are turned the employee will do as the boss does and not as the boss says. If the boss thinks it is right to appropriate things belonging to the business for personal use, even down to postage stamps and telephone calls, the employee may feel justified in doing the same. If the boss shortens his or her work day (takes an extra holiday now and then, attends to personal affairs during business hours, or slows down work and wastes business time), the employee may do likewise and not consider it dishonest.

When an employee actually steals cash or merchandise, the underlying fault may possibly be with management through its laxity in establishing proper safeguards and control over cash, stock, and supplies. Employees are people, and people are generally honest, but it is asking too much of the employee to expect him or her to always protect the employer's property if the employer fails to set an example by also doing so.

People enjoy doing interesting things, but an employee's work is often monotonous and uninteresting. Being human, they may seek an escape from monotony, thinking about and doing things other than their work when opportunities present themselves. They do not have the benefit of incentives that the boss has in pride of accomplishment and anticipation of profits. Perhaps they have nothing to look forward to but the same weekly pay envelope.

It is up to the boss to lead by example and to create a business atmosphere of systematic, smooth-running competency. The quality and efficiency of employee organization is but the reflection of its leader. The boss who blames staff for his or her troubles is simply proclaiming the employer's own incompetence.

"Do not mix friendship with business" is a warning commonly heard, but that applies more particularly to the asking of personal favors and not necessarily to being friendly with employees. A good boss does not fear being imposed upon and can enjoy and profit through such friendships because personal friendliness will not be permitted to swerve him or her from the straight line of good business procedure.

The days of "master" and "servant" in business have long since passed into history. Education and intelligence are now attributes of both employer and employee. The good leader leads and inspires employees by the employer's own example, by instilling a spirit of teamwork and cooperation, and by courteous "request" rather than "command."

11

Organization in Business

Business consists of providing goods or services to people. It may be just a few large goods or services, but generally it is a lot of smaller things or a mixture of many large and small goods or services in endless variety, from writing a letter or delivering a pound of coffee to moving a ton of freight.

The business owner's job and constant problem is to get these things done within the limits of time and cost that competition permits. In order to get the things done properly and promptly, a business needs organization.

One definition of **ORGANIZE** is "to bring into systematic relation, as parts of a whole." Business leaders use the words "organize" and "organization" in a number of ways, always associated, however, with "bringing together into systematic relation" the various elements and functions of business, as follows:

1. In starting a business, a person *organizes* it by bringing together ideas with ways and means of putting them into operation in preparation for transacting business.

2. If other persons are to participate, the owner brings these people together as the nucleus of a business *organization.*

3. The business relationship — the duties, responsibilities, and authority that each is to exercise, along with the detailed work routine

that each is to perform — is established by organizing the business operation.

4. The proprietor also *organizes* the work to be done personally, as
    well as the time made available each day for business purposes. The
    owner may *organize* the work of any department, sales, advertising, or
    production programs, or any other element of the business.

5. The business owner may also *reorganize*, from time to time, ele-
    ments that require new planning or a more efficient "system" of opera-
    tion. To *"systematize"* means the same as to *"organize."*

It is generally recognized that any business that is well organized as to per-
sonnel and work routine is a business that is efficiently managed. A business that
is efficiently managed cannot fail to be a prosperous business. Therefore, all
experienced business managers are constantly striving to improve the organization
of their businesses.

Some proprietors of small businesses are gifted with the ability to organize. They have well-ordered minds with the facility of readily fitting into a
smooth-working plan the varied details of their daily living and the elements of
their business. Many others do not know how to segregate and correlate the
various elements and put into effect a smooth-running operation.

One glimpse at the desk of some proprietors of small businesses will re-
veal interesting examples of this deficiency — piles of old and dusty bills, letters,
catalogs, and odds and ends of samples, parts and broken pieces tell only too
plainly that these business owners have never learned to organize their office
work. One wonders if other departments of their business follow this same
pattern.

Several million business activities are classified as "small businesses" —
concerns employing less than 100 people. Many of them would grow faster and

prosper better with a more comprehensive understanding and application of organization in business.

To classify further, there are:

1.   the small minority where the proprietor does all the things necessary to operate the business and therefore has no employees.

2.   the large majority, perhaps 80% of the total, that employ from two or three to 25 persons.

3.   the comparatively few larger concerns employing 25 or more, up to 100 employees.

With the first group, the need is limited to the proprietor organizing his or her own time and work, outlining what is to be done with each hour of the working day in order to attain maximum production and revenue from one's individual effort. An owner's sole stock in trade may be the hours of time wherein he or she can sell personal services to customers. If this time is not organized, the minutes and hours slip away and are lost. They are then unproductive and will yield no profit.

With the second group, there is the added need to organize the work routine of employees. It is not sufficient for the "boss" alone to be well organized and efficient in his or her work. The owner must be competent to plan and promote efficiency in the work others are to do.

The importance of this may be suddenly realized when the new proprietor is successful in solicitation of customers' orders and finds that the list of things to tend to has accumulated to more than he or she can personally attend to. The owner faces the problem of getting these things done in time to meet promises of delivery and, in a manner, to please the customer.

The owner needs the assistance of employees who have been properly instructed and trained. The owner also needs to be prepared with all the necessary materials, supplies, or tools that may be required to fill these orders. Anticipating these needs and providing for them is what planning and organizing in business means.

The ever-busy proprietor, harassed by a multitude of details, often is reluctant to take the time to properly train assistants. The owner must trust to verbal instructions that perhaps are given hurriedly and incompletely. There may be limited success, but chances are that much of the owner's precious time will be taken up correcting mistakes or repeatedly explaining what needs to be done. Such owners may also be quick to change or hire more help to get the work out, but the process of instruction must be repeated with each new employee, which, in the end, consumes more time.

The smart employer gets this job of instruction, training, and supervising of employees properly organized and reduced to a systematic procedure as early as possible, thus saving a lot of time and improving the efficiency of the organization.

Many small business owners complain that they cannot get any reliable help. Other owners operate successfully with the same general classification of employees and have no complaints. The reason for this difference, as many experienced employers know, is proper initial training, plus adequate supervision.

Employees generally appreciate having the opportunity to work where all details of business operation are governed by systematic procedure and routine. It gives promise of job security and advancement and is an incentive for their best effort. When new employees are started off with an explanation of the business and its organization, and a clear understanding of their duties is covered, as necessary, by detailed memoranda on work routine, the chances are in favor of such employees proving to be satisfactory and reliable.

Organization in business permits the proprietor to *run* a business. Without organization the business is generally *running the owner*. With business routine well organized and running smoothly, the proprietor has time *to think;* to pause long enough get a fresh viewpoint; to analyze the position of the business; to study market conditions and trends; to develop new plans for increasing sales; or perhaps for adding a new department or otherwise expanding the operation.

With renewed confidence in business ability, gained by successful progress in organizing the business, the proprietor feels secure in taking on more responsibilities with a larger staff of employees or associates.

The owner is progressing toward the third classification of "small businesses" consisting of those concerns employing 25 to 100 persons. These businesses were able to hold their position in the business world and grow larger because their proprietors recognized the value of proper organization. They realized the necessity of having others to assist in the administration and supervision if they were to have the size and kind of business that they wanted.

A corporal may drill and maneuver a squad, but even a general cannot maneuver a regiment without subordinate officers. As the business grows larger, the proprietor must apply the principles of organization to a higher echelon of assistants, who may be partners, shareholders, or selected employees. The proprietor may have started a business with someone to keep the books, or a supervisor over a group of operators or mechanics. Now the services of an office and credit manager, sales manager, warehouse supervisor, or factory manager may also be required.

All such positions entail responsibility and authority over those working under them. In their respective departments, these individuals represent and act for the "boss," carrying out instructions and coordinating their effort with that of other departments in accord with the policies and procedures the boss has laid down.

The boss, or chief executive, expects sub-executives to use the same good judgment the owner would use in the conduct of their respective departments; this means that each sub-executive must have an intimate knowledge of the policies and methods of work routine that the chief has established to govern various details of business operation and coordination among departments.

Picking the right person for the job is unquestionably important, but perhaps not so difficult when the chief has organized the work routine of each department, and has also set up instruction and training procedures for the individual filling the job.

This "bringing together into systematic relationship" all the various details of responsibilities, authority, and work routine, preferably in written memo form, is a valuable means of establishing a clear understanding between the leader and assistants.

The written memo or job description is always available when needed for reference. When a new department head is appointed, it enables this individual to get off to a good start with a guide to show what should be done and how it is to be done. The memo minimizes confusion and delay in attaining the desired efficiency in that department. Best of all, it saves time all around, and it eliminates misunderstandings, which are always costly.

It is common practice with larger business concerns to make up their own office manuals, charts, and routine work bulletins for a great variety of purposes. They may be designed to cover any phase of the business, from advising employees about working hours and company policies to elaborate charts governing production schedules.

"Big Business" could not do without these valuable aids in handling its tremendous volume of varied activities. Practice in the use of these symbols of organization will be valuable to any small business that wants to grow big.

ORGANIZE, DEPUTIZE, AND SUPERVISE

Many big and successful executives use the above caption as a slogan and basic rule for their administration.

First, the details of a business are segregated and *organized* into groups or departments.

Second, a qualified associate or employee is selected and *deputized* to assume responsibility for such department.

Third, the principal function of the executive then is to *supervise*.

Like a three-legged stool, no complicated business can stand if any one of these functions of administration is weak or missing. The boss must be proficient in all three.

12
The Function of Profit

The making of profit is the one incentive that puts individuals in business and keeps them interested in running a business for themselves. It is also common knowledge that all operating businesses are profitable, more or less. This is obvious, of course, as profit is the only source of funds from which to pay wages, salaries, taxes, and all business expense. There can be no other source. Therefore, profit is not only desirable, but indispensable.

No other factor receives as much thought and study from the established business owner. The business owner knows that profit does not come automatically, but only when the knowledge he or she has of the contributing factors that make profit possible is applied. How important it is then that the novice give time to studying how to make a profit; to discipline themselves to comply with the "rules" that others have found successful.

With such a variety of circumstances governing individual cases, one might say that profit is sometimes a happenstance or "luck," but business owners know that profit must be planned for and earned by doing the right thing at the right time.

Insufficient knowledge, carelessness, reckless decisions, excessive expenses, bad purchasing, and selling on too close a margin often cause a disappointing loss where a profit was anticipated.

Error is often made calculating profit as the difference between initial cost and selling price without deducting the operating expense involved. Such a figure is often fictitious and can easily be misleading.

Gross profit is never the *net* profit — the *real* profit for which an owner is striving. The net can only be approximated, yielding no true figure until all expense for any given period of time is deducted from the accumulated gross profit for such period.

Business owners estimate the amount of business they expect to do within a certain period and establish their "overhead" or fixed operating expense (rent, payroll, etc.). They try to keep expenses to a minimum to insure breaking even if business should not come up to their expectations. The objective, of course, is not only to achieve their sales estimate but to beat that figure to derive more profit. As volume, expense, and profit are always relative, constant effort is made to keep them in proper ratio.

Total sales for a given period generally consist of several transactions with different margins of profit, some in excess and some deficient in covering proportionate shares of operating expense. Careful analysis is always made to make sure the *average* margin of profit is sufficient. Short margin sales are held in check while encouraging the larger margin sales.

"Never pass up an opportunity to make a profit" is a common saying in business and generally good advice, but not always. Eager to build a large sales volume, a proprietor may reach out for new business knowing that the profit will be small, perhaps under the delusion that the bigger business will somehow make more money for him. Unless the owner figures the result carefully, he or she may eventually find that the new business was costly, wearing out equipment and earning less than when the smaller volume of business was done.

During the course of regular business, a proprietor may be offered an attractive order if he or she agrees to cut price below the customary figure. To do so may set up a precedent that may become embarrassing and a difficult situation to overcome later when the same customer comes back for more, or other customers find out about the lower price.

Or one may see a profit to be made by dabbling in something entirely foreign to the regular business. No objection, of course, to any transaction that turns out all right, but the old saying is, "A good shoemaker sticks to his last." Chances for success are generally better when a person sticks to the kind of business he or she knows best and gives it undivided attention.

13
The Purpose of Business Records

Many have tried to run a business without keeping books or accounting records and have succeeded about as far as one can keep track of time without consulting a clock and a calendar.

The keeping of accounting records is a definite responsibility of operating a business, and in many instances is required by law. It was not to satisfy government, however, that the keeping of records was invented way back in the days when individuals chiseled their business records on rocks. The practice came into being because the person in business had to know *facts* pertaining to the business in order to operate successfully — and so it remains today.

The need for record keeping is so universal that the rudiments of bookkeeping are taught to children in public schools. Everyone is expected to know something about it, and many do. But through lack of practice, there are very few who actually know how to apply the principles of bookkeeping to their own business when they begin for themselves.

Fortunately, facilities are easily available for acquiring the necessary knowledge and practice. There are plenty of books on the subject of self-instruction. There are day and evening courses in business schools. Proprietors of small businesses may make up any deficiency in this qualification at any time and almost anywhere. From the day of starting a business, an owner will require such knowledge.

A person may expect to have someone keep the company books but it is the responsibility of all proprietors to direct their bookkeepers, to say *what records they want kept, to say how they are to be kept, and how to use the information to the best advantage.*

It is, of course, always justifiable and advisable to have the assistance of a certified public accountant or a capable bookkeeper in the initial setting up of the books. Also, it is quite in order to employ someone to keep the accounts posted up-to-date if the proprietor is too busy with other elements of the business. Every good business owner has a working knowledge of the principles of accounting. The business owner who can get his or her own information quickly when needed from the records, kept smartly up to the minute, is generally the most successful in business.

BOOK RECORDS

The correct and proper system of bookkeeping for any business is the simplest system that will give the proprietor complete and accurate information when he needs it.

There are businesses so simple, and yet successful, that the person with "his office in a hat" may keep all essential records of business in a vest-pocket notebook. Others get by with notations made of their expenditures on the stubs of their bank checkbook. Such methods, however, are not considered adequate when speaking of business accounting records. Neither is it good business for anyone to try to memorize details of business transactions.

The time to start making written records of a new business is when the first money transaction is made for starting the business. A record of the financial facts at the beginning is important to any business. Continuing with each day's record thereafter is equally important.

The new business owner does not generally relish this daily "chore." There are so many more interesting things to do at the time that record keeping is considered less important and put off "until some other time." Procrastination often starts the bad habit of trusting to memory, and carelessness in keeping accounting records often results in running the business at a loss.

The first and most important record to keep is the *Cash Account*. This account is maintained to keep the proprietor informed as to all monies paid out and received — also to or from whom and for what.

The proprietor should know at all times how much money is obligated or spent for business expenses, how much money is invested in things to be sold, or in other things useful and needed in the business.

This information is made available by segregating the various expenditures and grouping the items together in supplementary accounts to be open on the company books. Bookkeeping systems that are in general use usually identify such accounts as follows:

1. The *Cash Account:* A general recording of all money received and paid out.

2. *Capital Account:* For recording the money put into the business for working capital (see also p.73) by the proprietor and any others.

3. *Notes Payable:* A separate record of loans contracted, when due, or when paid.

4. *Organization Expense:* While this is money spent when a business is starting, it is not a normal expense of operation. It is often put into a separate account to be disposed of later. Usually, organization expense is written off over a period of several years.

5. *Fixtures and Equipment:* The record of money invested in things for business use that will continue to have money value.

6. *Operating Expense:* The record that shows the cost of doing business, such as rent, light, heat, telephone, payroll, etc.

7. *Purchases*: Of stocks of merchandise, or materials, to be sold at a profit.

8. *Accounts Payable*: The record of what is currently owed to suppliers.

9. *Sales Account:* The daily record of customer sales.

10. *Accounts Receivable*: The account that shows what the customers still owe the business.

11. *Inventory:* The record that shows the money value of saleable stock on hand. A separate account shows value of fixtures and equipment (see #5 above).

12. *Profit and Loss:* The final account that shows whether or not the operation has been profitable or unprofitable for any particular period.

It is usually the function of the experienced bookkeeper or accountant to decide and recommend which of the above accounts are adaptable and required to any particular business, but it is always essential for the proprietor to have a clear understanding of the reasons for having them.

Whatever the system selected, the inviolable principle is that some record of the transaction must be made immediately. Business owners should not trust their own memory or that of their employees. No material or merchandise should be taken from the business without a receipt being obtained or some other record made.

The personal finances of the proprietor should always be kept strictly separate from the business finances, preferably by means of separate bank accounts, and always kept separately in the accounting records.

Whenever possible, all business bills are paid by check. Information regarding any expenditure is made on the check stub at the time the check is drawn, thus providing a record for future posting in the books. This check stub record is of value in verifying money transactions as well as keeping control of cash.

Frequently, errors will be found in the cash-on-hand figure. This often happens when money taken in is used to pay for minor expenses, instead of keeping all cash receipts strictly separated and putting them through the bank. Most businesses are in a position to deposit their receipts daily. This practice provides a daily record of sales as deposits. If other money is to be put in the bank, a separate deposit is made.

There may be a need for a small fund of cash on hand to be used to pay for postage, express charges, and various small items. This is best handled by anticipating the need of a certain amount of money for such purpose and drawing a check to *Petty Cash Fund* for such amount. Records of such minor expenditures are usually kept in a separate *Petty Cash Book*.

To further illustrate the need for the information obtainable from accounting or bookkeeping records, a few of the more important questions commonly asked by business owners follow.

- *"How much cash have we on hand?"* This is quickly answered by looking at the checkbook balance and adding the money in the cash drawer. Of course, if the proprietor has acquired the bad habit of carrying business money around in pockets, the answer may be, "Who knows?"

- *"How much money do our customers owe us?"* If there have only been a few charge sales made, the answer may be taken from the file of duplicate invoices, or *Charge Sale Slips*, or by reviewing the entries in the *Day Book*. If there have been several charge sales made, these items may be found listed in the ledger under the account labeled *Ac-*

counts Receivable. If the records have been kept posted up to date, it will not take long to get the answer.

Such records also give the important information as to whether or not such accounts are now due for collection. If due, and payment can be received, such additional money may help to meet the bills that should be paid today.

■ *"How much money does the business owe?"* and *"On what days are the different amounts due for payment?"* If the business has borrowed money and has a note to meet, the record is found in the ledger under *Notes Payable.* The date of acquiring the loan is there, from which the proprietor calculates the date when the company must have cash on hand to pay the loan. This is quite an important record to have and to keep correctly. All other long- and short-term obligations are also on record for the proprietor's information and financial planning.

Information on the amount owed for the current month's purchases and operating expense may have to be taken from the *Unpaid Bills* file. Many of these items are not recorded in the books until they are paid by check. If the proprietor has kept duplicate copies of his purchase orders, the owner may also know the additional amounts that have been obligated for payment before bills have been received.

■ *"How did our sales compare with the previous month?"* Most business owners are anxious to have this information quickly after the close of each month's business. The figures are in the ledger, or possibly in a separate *Sales Journal*, with each day's sales entered along with weekly or monthly totals added for quick comparison.

Purchases, too, are segregated or classified according to the need for specific information that the proprietor thinks will enable a better job to be done.

■ *"How much money have we tied up in materials or merchandise?"* The answer is found in the ledger under *Inventories*. Here is listed the cost value of what was first on hand, plus all succeeding purchases of such material.

At the close of each month, a physical inventory should be taken of what is left on hand by actually measuring or counting and appraising the value of such inventory. When these sums are added, the total figure is posted in the *Inventory* account in the opposite side of the ledger page to the previous figures. We now have the total cost of all that has been bought, and the value of what is still left.

The two figures will not be in balance because sales have been made. Some of the items on hand and those subsequently bought have been sold. The difference between the two figures, however, is very important information to the proprietor as it represents the *Cost of Goods Sold*. When this cost is deducted from the amount received (sales), the resulting figure is very important information — it is the *Gross Profit* (also called *Gross Margin*) for the period.

The *Gross Profit* is not all in the cash drawer or in the bank. In fact, it may have disappeared entirely. It has cost money to make these profits. This cost is called *Operating Expenses*.

■ *"What have the Operating Expenses been?"* If this expense account in the ledger has been kept smartly up to date, it will not take long to compute and find the total expenses for the month. Then this amount is deducted from the *Gross Profit* and the result brings either a smile or a frown. The result may show a nice *Net Profit* for the month, or it may show a *Loss*.

Whether profit or loss, this is essential information for the proprietor to have and to have as quickly as possible so that any necessary changes in the operation of the business can be made.

The various steps detailed in this chapter show how, by reference to re-cords, a *Monthly Operating Statement* — an invaluable guide to many successful business owners — is obtained. But it is obtainable only when adequate records are kept.

Suppose the records for the month show a nice net profit, but the bank bal-ance is alarmingly low instead of being comfortably adequate. *"Where did this extra money go?"*

The records are there with the answer. Turn first to *Inventories* to see if this extra money is invested in a larger stock of materials. If not there, examine the customers' accounts, *Accounts Receivable.* They may be higher than last month. Or it may be under *Furniture and Equipment,* in that new computer, display showcase, or shop equipment. Or perhaps *Notes Payable* will show that a loan has been paid off. Properly kept records can always be depended upon to give the correct answer.

It is not assumed here that every proprietor of a small business can get out a *Monthly Operating Report* without some assistance and still have it in time to do some good for the next month's operation. There are many other things to demand the boss's time and attention. But the owner must understand how this report is made and why the figures obtained are correct and dependable.

The really smart thing for the proprietor to do is to see to it that all records are kept up to date, to take the inventory carefully, and then to call in the account-ant to help compile the figures and analyze the results obtained. A friendly and competent accountant, or bookkeeper experienced in auditing work, may be regularly employed to make this monthly audit. Such a person is probably the most valuable personal aid any business owner can have.

14
The Use of Capital

Since money is the universal medium of operation, all businesses require the use of enough money to enable the proprietors to operate successfully.

The word "capital" is the business term used to distinguish between money that remains permanently tied up in the business from other monies that it handles. It is the money originally invested and all additional money put in from time to time as the business requires more of this commodity. Hence the term "working capital."

Capital serves certain well defined purposes:

1. *It pays for the requisites of business,* including office furniture, store fixtures, and perhaps a building, etc. Such things may be required, but that part of the capital is tied up indefinitely in these "frozen" assets.

2. *It pays for expenses of organizing the business,* for legal fees, expense of procuring capital, and bringing together necessary elements to get the business started.

3. *It buys the initial stock of merchandise or materials* the business is to sell. This is the important, productive usage of capital, and the major part of available funds is carefully reserved for this purpose. Capital here sets up a revolving fund. As money is received from sales, it relieves capital of this function, thus furnishing the means for replenishing stock.

4. *It pays for initial operating expenses* until sales can be built up sufficiently to produce enough gross profit which thereafter will be used to pay the operating expenses.

Another important function of capital is to carry the accounts receivable — money tied up in accounts owed to the business by its customers. In addition, money must always be available to keep the business supplied with things to sell, in the event customers do not pay cash. This portion of capital also becomes a revolving fund maintained by receipts from such customers.

It is the function of capital to supply money for investment in larger inventories and facilities as the business expands, to buy buildings or land, to put up a factory and equip it with machinery, and for all such purposes where the money is to remain tied up and therefore not available for other purposes.

This general purpose of capital is readily understood by all when applied to a very simple business. Money is used to buy a small stock of goods to be sold at a profit. When the goods are sold, the proprietor may take the *profit* from money received, but the owner must set aside the money originally invested as capital to buy more goods if the company is to continue in business. That is very simple, but many proprietors get into serious difficulties by confusing this issue when their businesses get more complicated.

Some start out with the idea that somehow the business will supply not only the profit they want to take out for their personal use, but also the capital funds the business requires to operate. They neglect to figure out just what the possibilities are. They generally overestimate the profits available after operating expenses are paid, and underestimate the amount of money the business will keep tied up as working capital.

Such money should be available first from the proprietor; second, from some other outside source; and lastly, from profits of the business, if and when accumulated in sufficient amount to be applied for that purpose.

Net profits after operating expense is paid are relatively small in most businesses, requiring considerable time to accumulate. Many and devious ways are figured out to circumvent the delay and procure those things which the proprietor considers necessary to the progress of the business. Temporary loans are obtained, or contracts entered into to buy expensive fixtures, tools, or equipment, without realizing the amount of capital funds needed to cover such commitments. When these notes or obligations become due for payment, the cash on hand that the business may have is diverted from its normal function to this use. Such errors multiply into many other financial troubles that often can only be overcome if and when capital funds become available.

When proper bookkeeping records are maintained, the proprietor is able to keep the financial affairs under proper control. With a clear understanding of the part capital plays in the business, plus the knowledge the bookkeeping accounts will supply to the owner, many difficulties may be avoided.

The proprietor can see from the records what part of the capital is gainfully employed and where it is being wasted or neglected, tied up in equipment, in stock that does not sell, or in overdue customers' accounts. By collecting these accounts and turning the stock and useless equipment into cash, such capital funds are released for more productive use.

It is the constant endeavor of good business executives to keep their capital as "liquid" as possible, i.e., available for use. Capital must be conserved and managed just as efficiently as other elements of the business. Business pays for the use of this commodity in interest or dividends. It should not be left lying idle, nor tied up in unproductive things.

It is not a simple matter for anyone to estimate the amount of capital a *new* business will require during its first few years. Good business judgment dictates that there must be sufficient capital to get the business properly started and to carry it through until sufficient sales volume has been built up, thereby producing sufficient gross profit to fully cover the operating expenses.

The amount required will vary according to conditions under which the business operates. In some, the need is related to seasonal volume of business done. All businesses require more and more working capital as they grow and expand.

15
Raising Capital

Unquestionably, the best way to start a new small business is for the person with the idea, and wishing to be the boss, to finance the venture out of personal funds. The business is then actually his or her own with no one to answer to for its success or failure.

It is generally imperative that some personal funds be available and used. Other people are not likely to invest where the proprietor is not assuming some financial risk. There are many instances, however, where individuals without a dollar of their own have started and developed successful businesses. So much depends on ability and the other qualifications of the person with the idea.

When a young person sets out to produce a few thousand dollars for a business venture, he or she may regard the matter simply as a problem of getting some friend or relative to lend the money, or the prospective owner may expect a bank to make the loan simply because he or she is willing to agree to pay it back. This would not be a wise attitude to adopt, nor the businesslike way of getting what is needed.

The procurement of money for use as working capital is an old institution of business, governed by long established rules and regulations that apply to all businesses from the smallest to the largest. Eventually all proprietors must learn the proper procedures for financing if they are to be successful. It is advisable to learn something about it at the beginning.

As previously explained, working capital is money more or less permanently invested in the business. It can be described as a certain "kind" of money in
the sense that it must be suitable for the purpose. For instance, a good friend may
have money saved through hard work and self-denial, put away as a safeguard
against some possible emergency. That is not the kind of money to solicit or
accept to help finance a business venture.

When money is invested in a business there is generally some element of
risk involved. All business owners generally accept that fact. Only the inexperienced are over-sanguine in their anticipation of all profits and no losses. It would
be poor business judgment, aside from showing a lack of moral rectitude, to
jeopardize the needed savings of a friend.

Therefore, business owners are particular as to the kind of money that is to
be employed as working capital. The business owner looks for money from those
whose business it is to supply it, or from those who can afford to take the normal
chances of a business investment.

Such money is generally available from individuals who have a surplus
above their immediate or emergency-related needs. Such funds may come from
the sale of property, cashing in of a mortgage, funds presently invested in stocks
not paying dividends, bonds with low interest return, or in some other asset. These
individuals may be interested in taking a normal risk in a business promising
better returns on their money.

The ability to make good profits in operating a business is a qualification
highly regarded by all who have surplus funds to invest. Many are looking for
opportunities to participate in such profits and prospective investors are generally
glad to listen to propositions that, in their own judgment, appear to be promising
and safe as investments.

Obviously there are right and wrong ways to approach a prospective investor. It would be wise before making any solicitation to test out the business
soundness of the proposition by getting the opinion of those more experienced. It

is not enough to demonstrate ambition, enthusiasm, and optimism for the proposed business. These fine qualities must be backed up by a carefully worked out proposal including all informative facts and figures relative to the proposition. The prospective investor may want the answers to such questions as the following:

1. What is the personal reputation or moral standing in the community of this person who wants me to put money into the proposed business?

2. Is the owner one who likes to gamble or speculate?

3. Does the owner know anything about running a business, about bookkeeping, purchasing, selling, or handling employees?

4. In what way has the owner proven his ability to operate any kind of business?

5. What has the owner garnered from actual experience about what is proposed to be done?

6. Has the owner shown that the proposed business is needed in the community? That is, is there a good market for what is expected to be sold?

7. Do the proposal and the figures demonstrate conservative business judgment in estimating the operating expenses?

8. How much personal money is the owner putting in?

9. Who else is investing money?

10. Has the owner carefully estimated how much capital will be needed?

It is well to be prepared to answer such questions and others. Above all, it is imperative to keep the matter strictly on a business basis, conducted throughout in a businesslike manner.

When a person has an idea for a sound business venture plus the ability to put it into operation, and another person has surplus money to invest, it is an opportunity for them to bring their combined resources together for their mutual benefit. Moreover, it should have all the necessary qualifications of a business transaction and is not a case of asking or receiving personal favors on either side.

There is the question, of course, of what the investor is to receive for his or her help in financing the business. Here may be the first test of the prospective proprietor's business judgment and foresight. If the prospective owner is over-anxious or impatient to get the business started, he or she very likely will offer · compensation for the use of the money far in excess of what is necessary, or of actual value to the business. If so, the owner is sure to regret it later. The owner may offer too large a share in the profits or in the ownership of the business. If it is to be in the form of a loan, he or she may offer too high an interest rate, or may promise to repay the loan at a time when possibly the money will not be available.

To be over-anxious to get your hands on other people's money is not a healthy situation to be in at any time, or for any reason. Besides, it's not business-like. It is better to take time to study business practices, and learn something of what people generally receive for supplying working capital for business, in the way of dividends and interest rates.

Personal time and effort, along with the ability to use money in a business to make money, is far more valuable than money itself. If the business prospers and grows, each share in the business grows more valuable year after year.

These things are to be kept in mind when bargaining with the investor for the use of money. In later chapters, the important subjects of partnerships, compensation for business associates, and business loans and debts are discussed more fully.

At some period after the business is started, it will probably require more working capital to finance the increasing sales. The proprietor will be fortunate at such time if the business has produced sufficient profits to provide a surplus that may be used for this purpose. If not, the proprietor must again seek outside investors.

It is often puzzling to business owners to learn that banks and most other money-lending concerns are not interested in loans for capital investment. The reason for this is that such money is to be tied up more or less permanently in larger inventories, equipment, and/or added facilities. Such loans can only be repaid when there are other capital funds available for the purpose.

Banks are required by federal and state regulation to keep depositors' money more or less readily available to the depositor, which generally limits bank loans to short-term, or temporary loans, generally made against negotiable security. There are exceptions to this rule but this is the general practice.

Procuring additional working capital for a going business is generally less of a problem than for a new business. Much depends, however, on the proprietor's understanding and manner of solving it. Capital will not come without a solicitation. The owner has a job to do, one of the most important in the operation of the business and worthy of the best thought and careful attention, calling for adequate preparation and some salesmanship.

The proprietor first makes careful analysis of the operation to date, reviewing what has been accomplished with the capital available to work with. The owner scrutinizes each instance in which capital is now employed, searching for money that may be currently tied up unproductively. If found, the owner takes steps immediately to convert such investments into cash. The owner does not go out looking for more capital when it can be culled from the business.

The business owner reviews operations profit-wise. He or she analyzes the extent to which it has really been profitable, or whether it has existed by consuming its own working capital. Has the gross profit been too small to cover the operating expense, or has the owner permitted operating expenses to exceed profit? Obviously, it would be foolish to "throw good money after bad" if the business has not proven to be profitable to some degree.

Assuming no such objectionable conditions exist, the proprietor will be able to show that the business has been well managed, that it is now a going concern doing a profitable business, that valuable customer goodwill has been built up, and that the future prospects are excellent. Essential facts and figures demonstrating these qualifications for additional investment are taken from the accounting records and compiled into two standard reports commonly used by all businesses.

1.   *The Financial Statement* lists informatively the *assets* and *liabilities* of the business. It shows what the business owns in cash on hand or in things of equivalent value listed as *Assets*, and what debts or other obligations the business has listed as *Liabilities*.

2.   *The Income Statement* or *Profit and Loss Statement* shows completely but concisely the transactions of the business, dollar volume of sales, cost of goods sold, gross profit, operating expenses, and finally, the net profit earned.

As such reports are commonly used and required by banks when application is made for short-term business loans, it is important for businesspeople to become thoroughly familiar with, and proficient in, compiling such reports. Add to these sources of information also a memorandum describing future prospects, plans for developing new markets, and ideas for increasing sales. In addition, show plans for affecting economies in operating that will result in greater profits, and the prospective investor will be in a position to appraise the soundness and desirability of the proposed investment.

If it is to be a long-term loan to the proprietor with returns being made in periodic installments, the financial statement will show what, if any, prior loans or obligations may take precedence over this new loan. Also, the financial statement will show liquid assets available for contingencies. The operating statement should show that the business is sufficiently profitable to insure the amortization and interest payments being made without developing undue strain on the finances of the business.

If the money is to be put into the business in exchange for ownership shares or stock, the investor will want to know what he or she may expect to receive from the investment. Surely the investor is entitled to something for the use of his or her money, particularly if the investor is asked to exchange it for stock that may not be readily saleable in the open market.

It is presumed that the executive head of the business (heretofore called the "proprietor") intends to continue to direct the business and, therefore, is retaining the *majority* interest or *control* of the business. The proprietor is offering a *minor* share, which gives the investor no rights to dictate to management as to the handling of such money.

Armed with this knowledge, the investor will base the decision to invest upon confidence in the proprietor to continue to manage the business, such confidence being strengthened by the prior record of accomplishments.

The potential investor will want to know what dividends to expect. If the operation shows generous dividends consistently paid, the question is answered. If no dividends have been paid, what have the original investors received so far as a reward for furnishing the working capital?

This question is also answered in the operating and financial statements. If the statements show that the business has been exceptionally profitable, with such profits being retained or reinvested in the business, it will be evident that money originally invested is now represented by greater assets. Shares in the business have become more valuable. If this is the case, the investor may be satisfied to forego dividends for a time and make the investment in anticipation of enhancement in the value of the shares.

Notwithstanding stockholders' willingness to continue without receiving dividends, the executive must keep in mind the importance of establishing a good record of dividend payments. Shares may continue to increase in book value, but the stockholder may still have difficulty in finding a buyer if wishing to sell. The majority of investors are interested in receiving consistent returns on their investments.

When the proprietor of a small business is not so fortunate as to have very favorable financial and operating records to attract the investor, the proprietor need not give up looking for the capital the business needs. There may have been extenuating circumstances and conditions that have prevented more successful operation so far.

The company's prospects for the future may be very bright. The proprietor may be able to show that valuable customer goodwill has been built up and have proof of an ability to organize and manage business. All businesses are not profitable all the time, but good management is always worth investing in.

16

The Business Plan

Despite bootstrapping, help from relatives, etc., the new enterprise may need additional capital from venture capital sources or sophisticated investors or lenders. In such cases, it is imperative for the entrepreneur to prepare a detailed business plan.

The business plan is a great deal of work. Careful preparations of a business plan can be very beneficial to the entrepreneur preparing to launch a new business venture. A business plan helps the entrepreneur see what resources (human, physical, and monetary) are needed for the proposed venture. The business plan is also a useful tool for seeking financing for the new enterprise if outside funding is necessary from professional investors or lenders. The business plan is a vehicle that outlines why the business venture is a good opportunity for an investor or lender. The business plan must state in writing the key factors in the proposed new venture. The plan should describe succinctly the product or service offered by the new enterprise. Problems as well as prospects should be disclosed.

Generally, it is best to begin the business plan with a section on the proposed product or service, the company, and the industry. The product or service should be described fully in nontechnical language. There should be a brief description of others in the industry and how the new company will fit into this industry.

A second section should be prepared on the management of the proposed new enterprise. This section should include an organization chart for the company and descriptions of the backgrounds of all key members of the management team. It should include information on supporting professional services and outside members (if any) comprising the board of directors.

The third section of the business plan is often a detailed section on market research and analysis. This section describes the current market and projected market trends for the product or service to be entered. A list of all competition and their estimated share of the market is included here.

Following the section on market research and analysis should be a section on the marketing plan for the new enterprise. This section should include details of the marketing channels the new product or service will use (direct selling, use of distributors, etc.), a sales plan, and a service plan. This will include plans for developing new products or applications in the future, if any.

If the new enterprise is involved in manufacturing, a manufacturing plan should be developed as a section of the business plan. This part of the plan would include a production schedule. If the new enterprise provides a service, an operation plan and a schedule for how and when the service is to be performed should be included in this portion of the plan.

A key section of the business plan is one outlining the risks in the proposed new enterprise. This section is important so that potential investors will know the management has recognized the possible risks facing the new enterprise. This area should encompass an evaluation of how serious the risks are and what contingency plans have been established in the event that the risks actually occur. For example, one risk is that sales forecasts are not achieved. An evaluation of this risk will show what margin, if any, exists between breakeven level and sales forecasts to provide a cushion. Contingencies for lower sales than forecast might include a cutback in purchasing or a reduction in staff.

A financial plan for the new enterprise is an important and necessary section of the business plan. A five-year financial forecast based on the marketing outlook should be prepared. Pro formula income statements, balance sheets, and cash flow forecasts for each year can be prepared, listing all assumptions used. Breakeven charts are often helpful.

The final section of the business plan should be a section on funds to be raised and how they are to be raised. For example, a new enterprise may need $300,000 in capital. The entrepreneurs may provide one hundred thousand dollars. This should be detailed, along with how many shares each of the entrepreneurs will receive in return. The remaining $200,000 may be provided by investors in exchange for a certain number of shares of stock, or by lenders in exchange for a note, perhaps with stock options.

The business plan is a helpful tool to the entrepreneur in raising money to start up, buy, or expand an enterprise. The entrepreneur must decide between debt and equity (or a combination) and sources include wealthy investors, venture capital firms, public stock offerings, private placements, the Small Business Administration, state government agencies that help develop new business, trade credit, banks, finance companies, factors, and leasing companies. If the new enterprise is to be organized as a partnership, limited partners can be considered as well. Often, the potential investor, after reading the business plan, will call upon the entrepreneur to make a presentation of the plan in person. The entrepreneur may be fortunate enough to have several willing investors and then must make a choice.

Once funding for the new enterprise has been secured, the company can be started up. It is helpful to the entrepreneur to lay out all the steps necessary to start up the new company in advance of actually starting it up. Again, major problems should be anticipated, such as length of time to secure a corporate charter and regulatory approval from government agencies if needed. When will the members of the management team be available to begin work?

The entrepreneur must also think of his or her ultimate goals. If the new enterprise is very successful, what does he or she ultimately seek? They may choose to remain with the business, taking out a good return in salary and dividends. Stock may be sold to employees or other managers through stock option plans or a management buyout. The company may be merged with another company. The assets can be sold or the company may "go public" through a stock offering. Any of these positive alternatives may occur after many years of hard work.

17

Business Loans and Debts

To buy and sell on a cash basis exclusively is always good sound business. This policy is strongly recommended for small businesses because of the many advantages in simplicity of operation, saved time, greater financial safety, and general aid to business efficiency. Those individuals who have sufficient funds in their own right to finance their enterprise, and whose businesses are of a nature to permit cash operation, are in an enviable position in the business world.

But every *business* is in debt, if only to the proprietor for the money the proprietor has invested in the business.

Indebtedness is a normal element of business generally — indebtedness to people who have invested money — indebtedness for current purchases of merchandise, materials, and supplies; and indebtedness for current monthly operating expenses. Businesses that are operated on a cash basis exclusively are a small minority.

Therefore, it is a highly important function and responsibility of management not only to know how, but to keep all business indebtedness under strict control and within its proper sphere. This is not at all a simple task under the various vicissitudes of business. To fail to realize the importance of this element of business can be a source of trouble for small businesses.

"Big Business" employs the services of highly trained experts and specialists in various branches of business indebtedness to handle its intricate problems

of financing. It is not the purpose of this book to discuss the problems of *"Big Business,"* but to help the small business owner over the simpler but equally important difficulties.

The first debt that a business acquires is for the money invested in it. In a small business this presents no particular problem if this money is invested by the proprietor out of personal funds. If the money is lost through mismanagement of the business or any other cause, the proprietor has no one to answer to but himself or herself.

However, many businesses are started on borrowed money and may need additional loans from time to time. Much depends on how loans are negotiated as to whether the new business is going to get off to a good start and survive, or come to an early end.

The young person undertaking a first business venture and needing capital quite naturally thinks first of relatives or friends as possible sources of capital for the business. However, it is not good practice to seek a business loan on the basis of a personal favor. Loans must always be negotiated in strict conformity with good business practice, and considered by both parties to be a business proposition rather than a personal matter.

It is wise to acknowledge that the new proprietor with limited experience may make some mistakes in "guestimating" the amount of capital the business will require to carry it through its formative period, or the extent to which operating expenses will consume the business profits, out of which the loan is eventually to be repaid. In an enthusiasm for the new venture, the proprietor may commit to obligations for repayment of a loan, which may be too much of a burden on the business. The new proprietor may also overestimate the proper value of such a loan, agree to pay too much for the use of such money either through assignment of an interest in the business or too large a share in the profits.

Such mistakes, when capital is invested by friends or relatives, often result in family dissension or loss of valuable friendships, which is not going to be helpful to the new business. They may also cause discouragement and failure of an otherwise promising business career.

Consequently, it is important that this first step in business finance be taken cautiously and with the realization that borrowing and lending money in business is a radically different matter from transactions applying to personal finances.

BUSINESS LOANS

No business loan should be negotiated before obtaining a clear understanding of the simple but absolute factors that govern this important element of business. Information on the subject is generally available in almost any city or town and may be readily acquired in a few hours time.

It is the business of commercial banks, finance companies and the Small Business Administration to lend money to business. Since that is the principal source of their revenue, they generally want all the good business loans they can get, thus it is part of their business to offer all necessary information on loan requirements. Some will take pains to explain reasons and also give valuable financial advice.

The bank's business of lending money to business is long established and practices have been well standardized. Laws provided to safeguard the bank's depositors, whose money it is that the bank lends to business, regulate loan requirements. These requirements, the principles of which apply equally well to loans made by individuals, apply to the two basic elements of all loans:

■ assurances of repayment

■ terms and conditions

Assurances of repayment is more than a person's promise to pay. There are many reasons for this without questioning the borrower's integrity. The uncertainties of life are always a factor, and notwithstanding the owner's willingness, some happening beyond the borrower's control may make him or her financially incapable of repaying the loan on that future date when it becomes due. Consequently, the question must be asked: "What security is offered?"

Security may be things tangible or intangible, or a combination of both. Tangible security, often called "collateral," is any real or personal property that the borrower possesses that he or she may be willing to assign to the lender temporarily until the loan is repaid. The appraised money value of such "collateral" should be adequate to cover the amount of the loan. A great variety of property is usable for such purpose, from real estate to personal jewelry, stocks, bonds, life insurance, or rights to money due the borrower from customers or other sources.

It is the policy of commercial banks generally to accept only certain classifications of property as security. This is one of the restrictions imposed on them by banking laws. Lending companies and individuals may accept other security.

To assign property as security does not mean that the lender has title to the property, nor is it necessarily given into the lender's possession, but the lender does have a claim or a "lien" against property so assigned and it cannot be transferred to another until the lien is satisfied by the repayment of the loan. If the loan is not repaid when it is due, the lender can claim the property. Almost invariably, banks and other lenders do not want to have to claim the property assigned as security. They only want it to fulfill its purpose — to guarantee repayment of the loan.

On the other hand, there have been instances where the lender, either bank or individual, has taken advantage of the borrower's inexperience and has deliberately placed the borrower in a bad financial position through making a loan which was known to be beyond the capacity of the borrower to repay. Valuable securities, real estate, or business assets, pledged as collateral for such loans, have been grabbed legally the moment payment became delinquent. This cannot happen if the borrower is prepared and pays the loan promptly on the due date; but the fact that it is *liable* to happen must be kept in mind when negotiating any loans.

When one is over-anxious to obtain money, there maybe a tendency to become careless as to terms and conditions of a loan. There is no obligation on the part of the lender to "wet nurse" the borrower. Sympathetic consideration has no place in business money transactions and business is quite ruthless and cold-blooded in penalizing carelessness.

When personal property, merchandise, furniture, equipment, etc., are assigned as security, the usual practice is to execute a *Chattel Mortgage* in favor of the lender, which is simply a different form of assignment.

Sometimes banks make loans to business without security when a good credit rating has been established with the bank. As a substitute for the assignment of property as security, the bank is given other substantial assurances that the amount of the loan can be recovered from the business. To establish this credit rating, the borrower files with the bank a written and certified statement listing all business possessions of value as well as all business debt and other financial obligations. From this financial statement showing all assets and liabilities, the banker learns the true financial condition of the borrower's business and decides whether the loan can be repaid. The financial statement also helps determine the amount of the loan to be granted.

In addition, there is another form of intangible security that is considered important by the lender. That is the personal reputation of the borrower, the confidence the borrower has inspired in the ability as a businessperson to operate the business profitably. The bank considers the borrower's conservatism as against the propensity to speculate and take undue business risks and also the record of the borrower for fair and square dealings.

In order to put the business in the enviable position of having a good credit rating with the bank, the proprietor of a new small business becomes acquainted with the local banker at the earliest opportunity. The owner does not wait until the business is in urgent need of a loan. The owner discusses business plans with the banker and tells the banker, frankly, the owner's true and exact financial condition.

This acquaintanceship is not difficult to make. The banker will most probably welcome the owner as a prospective customer for the bank. The banker will certainly appreciate receiving the visit and keep the information on file, and will frequently impart some valuable information and advice on business financing.

It may take time to build up a credit rating. In addition to filing financial statements, some loan transactions may transpire between the business owner and the bank. This will probably come about through a small and conservative loan being made and promptly paid when due. At a later date, another loan may be made and is promptly paid, and so on. Meanwhile, a satisfactory bank balance should be maintained. As this record grows, a satisfactory basis for negotiating future loans is developed.

When the lender requests an *endorser* or *co-signer*, it simply means that the borrower is not considered a good financial risk by himself. The lender wants another person with better financial standing to assume or share the obligation of repayment of the loan.

It may be justified in some instances to request someone to endorse a note in order to procure a loan that cannot otherwise be obtained, but this practice is very unpopular with businesspeople in general. It is bad for both parties. When a person endorses a note, he or she becomes both borrower and lender himself, usually without compensation for his or her trouble or for the liability he or she has assumed. It affects the co-signer's own credit rating, as well as the borrower's. Rather than endorse the loan, he or she might better lend the money himself. Many of those inexperienced in business do not realize the magnitude of the favor they ask when they request another to become a co-signer or endorser.

Terms and conditions may vary with each business loan made. The lender will consider the amount of the loan and the value of the security. There are "gilt-edge" loans and loans where considerable financial risk is involved.

A prerequisite of all loans is the *interest rate* — the cost the borrower pays for the use of money. The *interest rate* is always agreed upon between the lender and the borrower at the time the loan is made. Such rates vary from 3% to 15% per annum, with the majority of business loans being at the prime rate plus one or two percent. The U.S. government generally pays less than business, but such loans are valued higher than all others because of the surety of repayment.

Experienced business owners are, of course, quite familiar with established interest rates, but the inexperienced are prone to set too high a value upon the use of money, particularly when they require a few thousand dollars to start in business.

There is hardly ever any justification for paying an exorbitant rate of interest or other premium for a loan. If the new proprietor will have the patience to proceed more slowly and with greater caution, he or she very likely will find that they can get through without requiring the costly loan.

While the borrowing of money for business use is a desirable and necessary element of business, no good, small businessperson borrows money when the business can do without it. The owner will borrow money to make money, in a clever purchase of merchandise or materials, or to refinance another debt more economically, but at the same time, the owner will strive to avoid the burden of paying interest and of having to show this debt on a financial statement. Consequently, good business practice, at least for the small business, dictates that the amount of borrowed money be kept down to the absolute minimum with as little expense for interest as possible.

The *period of time* for which the loan is obtained will, of course, vary with the nature of the loan, and with the security that is given. Business loans with banks are usually negotiated for terms varying from ten to ninety days. Sometimes they may be extended or renewed, but very seldom are they permitted to run in excess of one year.

Obviously, the timing of repayment of the loan must coincide with the expected availability of funds. One does not borrow for ninety days unless one has carefully planned beforehand to be in a position to pay the money on the date specified.

Terms and conditions may also provide for amortization of the loan, that is, for repaying in installments. In such cases it is customary, but not always necessary, to have a series of notes (one for each payment) instead of a note for the entire amount.

There is a good deal of similarity here to a *conditional sale* agreement, whereby purchase is made of an expensive piece of equipment, with deferred payment in installments. Much business is done on this basis, and all such agreements to govern such purchases are assumed business debts.

The smart businessperson, knowing that all such business debt payments must come out of business profits left over after other bills and operating expenses are paid, does not require the business to make burdensome payments.

CURRENT OPERATING DEBTS

Successful business owners pay their bills for current monthly purchases and operating expenses "on the button" and with strict regularity. They can do it because they use foresight and planning. Hit or miss operators soon find that they are not doing well on their credit rating with their suppliers or other business connections.

Payrolls must be met promptly, usually weekly and on a certain day of the week. Utilities are generally paid monthly, with a definite date being set aside. Purchases of merchandise and commonly used materials are paid for in accordance with the purchasing terms and conditions.

Much business is done, however, on the basis of monthly settlement and good business practice dictates that all such monthly accounts be paid by check on or before a certain day of each month, generally the 10th.

Many suppliers offer a *cash discount* for settlement in ten days, thereby allowing time for the monthly statement to arrive and invoices to be checked. But the cash discount allowance is for settlement strictly according to terms, on or before the 10th, and not the 11th or the 12th or some time later.

The smart business owner never fails to pay suppliers promptly and regularly, and the owner never neglects to take the *quick* and *sure profit* of the *cash discount.* It may appear to be a very minor item in itself, but it amounts to a tidy sum on the entire year's purchases.

OLD DEBTS

If a business is burdened with a debt that seems to be a special problem, it may require the advice or services of an experienced accountant or the friendly service of a banker. These two specialists are familiar with problems of various kinds of businesses and can point the way out of a business difficulty that the proprietor may not be able to see.

Many businesses have debt problems. Some are old debts that have lingered a long time. Some are inflicted upon the business by unavoidable circumstances. Some, as proprietors must admit, may be due to careless management. Unfortunately, it is quite common for proprietors having trouble paying their way to resort to alibis and excuses instead of facing the fact of their own mismanagement.

Businesspersons get into mental ruts and sometimes an explosion is needed to jolt them. A debt problem that could be resolved easily has them hogtied. Like *Sinbad the Sailor* with the *Old Man of the Sea* on his back, they cannot seem to shake it and get back on the smooth road of good management.

"I can't pay my bills because I can't get my customers to pay me!" This is an old and common alibi as full of holes as a sieve. Instead of telling others this sad tale, the owner should drop the first half of the sentence and add the word "why" to the last half: *"Why can't I get my customers to pay?"* Then let the owner think carefully about it.

Why admit an inability to do what every person who runs a business must learn to do. Collect! That's the answer. Get out and collect what's due from the customers! Then pay what you owe others.

There must be no vacillating in applying good business judgment to this important element of business. A firm policy must be established and consistently maintained. This begins with strict adherence to approved rules of credit when charge sales are permitted. Then, follow through with courteous reminders in order that customers do not forget that they are expected to pay promptly. Customers usually respect such an established policy and will generally abide by it.

"I can't pay because I have to use the money to meet notes on new equipment." This is a clear case of confused financing. This person has overburdened the business with equipment that usually requires added capital investment. Evidently, the owner was either reckless in buying or overestimated the capacity of his business to furnish the money required to make this capital investment. Actually, the owner is appropriating money rightfully belonging to suppliers or other creditors to pay the notes for new equipment. The way out of this one is to refinance the equipment payments by having them stretched out over a longer period of time.

The proper procedure is to go to the creditors promptly and frankly explain the situation, which is not a new or unusual one in business. The people who sold the equipment probably have had other similar cases and may consider themselves partly to blame in setting up the terms of the payment. They generally prefer not to reclaim the equipment and most likely will be glad to cooperate with the debtor in working out a more practical refinancing plan.

"I can't pay because I had to pay off the mortgage on my house," or *"I can't pay because my wife has just had an expensive operation."* Here, the proprietor has failed to recognize the business as being a separate entity from personal affairs. No doubt this person's business is a fairly prosperous one, quite capable of paying its way and regularly providing income for the proprietor. But the owner has saddled it with the extra burden of providing a substantial lump sum for the owner's private needs when the business does not have enough surplus funds. This is a good way to kill the goose that lays the golden egg!

Instead of taking such a large sum of money out of the business, with the result of inconveniencing creditors and jeopardizing the credit standing of the business, it would have been better judgment to arrange for a personal loan to take care of these personal obligations.

It may have been excusable in the case of a sickness emergency to have used the business money temporarily until the personal loan could be arranged. In paying off the house mortgage, it is questionable that an emergency existed. Real estate mortgages are usually subject to refinancing and if so, in this case, it would have been better judgment to have the mortgage extended and not attempt to pay off the entire balance at one time.

"I can't pay because business is bad." Another common excuse. How bad is business? Why is it bad? Is it temporarily or permanently bad? What is the proprietor doing to make it better? Many businesses have periodic or seasonal slumps. The better plan is to prepare for such dull periods by building a reserve when business is good.

If business is bad generally, it may also be bad with the creditors whose capital is tied up with other delinquent dealers as well. Their businesses may also be endangered. When this unfortunate condition exists (perhaps due to bad weather conditions where the business is seasonal) a good plan is for those who are "all in the same boat" to get together and cooperate in their efforts to help each other over the difficulty.

In any instance where a debt cannot be paid when due, the right and good business thing to do is to go promptly to the creditor and explain the circumstances. It is quite probable that the creditor's plans require the use of this money to meet the creditor's own obligations, and it is grossly unfair to mislead the creditor into thinking the debt will be paid any day, where there is no assurance when it will be paid. The creditor is entitled to whatever information is available to assist him or her in preventing the upset of his or her own business projects.

Creditors are the same people in business that they were before the debt became overdue. They may become irritated by the poor business judgment shown by the debtor or in the attitude or manner in which the owner handles obligations. Almost invariably they will appreciate knowing the circumstances and will give valuable assistance in pointing the way to clear the debt.

In any case of chronic business debt, it will generally help the proprietor if he or she can get far enough away from the business to see where its various components are out of balance. Something is obviously wrong and has caused the business debts to get out of control. It must be brought back and debts kept within their proper sphere, even if such drastic measures as winding up the business and starting anew are necessary. Most individuals, eventually successful in business, have lived through one or two unfortunate ventures, but each one taught them some lesson in business management that was vitally important to their ultimate success.

18
The Use of Credit in Business

Before launching one's business on the sea of credit, one must learn something about its navigation. Many businesses have foundered because the pilot did not know what course to lay and ventured too far from the safety of a cash-in-hand policy.

When one buys for cash and sells for cash, the elements of the transactions are comparatively simple; but when one buys with intent to pay later, or sells with payment deferred, the transaction may become quite involved unless the principles of business pertaining to credit usage are known and strictly complied with.

Credit is universally in use, and because of its great value to all commerce and industry, experienced and successful business owners are most careful not to disrupt its even flow. The rules of credit are the result of hard won experience of generations of trade and commerce. They are accepted by businesspersons everywhere and are not to be trifled with. More failures of small businesses are traceable to noncompliance with the accepted rules of credit than to any other factor.

The usage of credit must be learned from two angles: One pertains to its use by the proprietor in purchasing, procuring loans, and other matters where the business itself is the *debtor*. The other angle is where the business sells to its customers on terms other than cash. The business then becomes the *creditor*.

When a capital loan is accepted, a stock of goods purchased on credit, or equipment bought with payments deferred, the proprietor automatically obligates the company to comply with the rules of credit governing such transactions, which the proprietor presumed to know.

Before so obligating the company, the proprietor must work out a plan for paying this business debt if incurred, and be reasonably sure that the company will have the necessary funds on hand to meet each and every payment.

Credit is extremely sensitive, and the least infraction of the rules may result in a serious handicap to the business. Excuses may be listened to and accepted, but the infraction will not be forgotten.

Credit is also very generous, and not difficult to deal with when the rules are known and complied with. Every businessperson has the opportunity to build up the valuable asset of a "credit rating" for the business. Such rating is generally based on the three C's of credit: *Capacity*, *Character*, and *Capital*.

Capacity is concerned with the business's buying record, amounts, punctuality, and regularity of payments. *Character* pertains to the businessperson's "moral" standing, his personal reputation for integrity and fair dealing. *Capital* pertains to the net financial worth of the business investment.

Obviously, one starting a first business will not have a complete credit record in all three of the above categories. He or she will able to build up their "capacity" for buying and paying for what is purchased only if some supplier is willing to provide the company goods on credit, based on the reputation of the owner or endorsement of a third party. It is then that the new proprietor must be on guard to see that no careless error is made that may put a blot on the credit record. As the owner continues to buy and meet obligations with regularity, the record is built up and increased in value to the business.

Frequently, the proprietor of a new business is offered more credit than expected, and he or she may feel flattered by salespeople competing for such patronage. This is a situation requiring determination to resist. Too liberal credit creates the temptation to buy more than was originally planned, thus producing a large stock of merchandise when the proprietor has not yet had the opportunity to learn which items will sell readily and which will remain on the shelves unsaleable (this is called an "overstock"). If this temptation is not resisted, it may result in the business being encumbered with unnecessary debt and depletion of capital that can seriously endanger its success.

Everyone wants to make the best possible impression on the public when the business is opened, and the temptation is great to buy fine looking office furnishings, store fixtures, or complete and elaborate equipment when the requisites are freely offered on credit terms.

Such offers of credit on equipment are not particularly complimentary to the buyer as such sales are usually made under *Conditional Sale Agreements*. The seller retains title, or ownership, until the last payment is made. The seller may, and generally does, enter and remove the seller's property if payments are not maintained.

In some rare instances, there may be an opportunity to buy on credit with the privilege of returning unsold merchandise. This is literally doing business on someone else's capital. There have been occasions where the wholesaler, or manufacturer, permits the retail dealer to return or exchange slow-moving or obsolete items, with the account being carried on a credit basis. Obviously, this does not happen unless the dealer's credit record is excellent.

Usually, when merchandise is left with the dealer to be sold, without obligation to pay unless sold, it is covered by a *Consignment Agreement*. Such arrangement is useful at times since it exposes certain articles to the possibility of sale when the dealer does not want the risk of buying them. The owner retains title and right to repossess this property if not sold, and the dealer agrees to pay the owner promptly when and if sold.

Credit standing enters into all such business transactions, and the successful business operator is scrupulously careful not to abuse such privilege. For instance, the business operator would not divert money received from a consignment sale to other purposes instead of paying the seller promptly. Promptness in meeting financial obligations of whatever sort is essential to building a good credit rating.

National and local credit information agencies exist to serve commerce and industry in the handling of the vast amount of business that is done on a credit basis. One or more of such agencies will probably know about the new business being started before it is even announced to the public. Some wholesaler, or supplier, will want to learn something about the individual behind the new enterprise and contact the agency whose service is subscribed to in order to obtain the information.

Every person operating a business needs to know something about these agencies and how they operate, as it is to the proprietor's advantage to work with them rather than ignore them.

A salesperson finds an opportunity to sell a bill of goods to a retail dealer who requests that the order be filled on an "open account" basis; i.e., goods to be delivered and payment to be made later. The salesperson may ask the new dealer-customer two things. First, he or she may ask for *credit references* — the names of three concerns that have more or less regularly supplied the dealer on open account. Secondly, he or she may ask that a statement of the dealer's business financial condition be sent to the company that will be supplying the material with deferred payment.

It is the salesperson's duty to explain the reason for the company wanting this information, and also to advise the buyer that a few days' time may be required to formally "open" the account, thus causing some delay in shipping the order.

When the customer's order reaches the salesperson's home office with credit reference names given, the bookkeeper or credit manager simply reaches for a small pad of printed forms, tears off three identical slips and mails one to each of the three names given as references. The confidential information that the reference is asked to furnish is covered by brief answers to three questions printed on the slips:

1. How long has the customer been sold on open account?
2. What is the highest amount of credit recently given?
3. Does the customer pay promptly and regularly?

A glance at the answers received is usually sufficient for the new supplier to decide whether or not he or she also wishes to extend open account terms to that dealer-customer. If the answers show that the dealer's paying habits are good, there is little doubt that the open account will be granted.

Millions of dollars of credit business is granted using this simple procedure between many thousands of dealers and suppliers, resulting in a general feeling of confidence inspired by the many years that this service has successfully functioned.

Various trade associations also operate *credit bureaus*, providing credit information to their members that is pertinent to certain fields of business.

There are also credit investigating concerns. The largest is Dun and Bradstreet — a long-established, reputable house, whose services are subscribed to by thousands of suppliers. This concern has representatives most everywhere who call on local businesses with requests for information on their financial status. This is often done because one of their subscribers may want to sell the dealer on credit and has asked Dun and Bradstreet for a dealer's *credit rating*. In some exceptional cases, Dun and Bradstreet will also make special investigations and furnish detailed reports to their clients. Dun and Bradstreet publishes a large directory listing many thousands of businesses, large and small, in every city and town. The directory assigns to each firm a *credit rating* in confidential code. These ratings are based upon information on file pertaining to the financial strength and business record of individuals and firms.

Successful business owners are generally proud of their "D&B" rating. There are some businesspeople who resent being questioned about their business's financial condition by "D&B" investigators. Or, they may think they are better off if they try to conceal a weakness in the financial position of their business. Such attitudes generally hinder their own progress, since many suppliers rely extensively on Dun and Bradstreet ratings before granting credit.

Such confidential information is never given out indiscriminately, unless it is to serve the definite purpose of establishing credit where credit may be desired. There is nothing to fear from giving such information to those who are accredited to receive it. The business world is too actively engaged with serious matters to indulge in any "Prying Paul" pastime. It is only interested in seeing that every business helps and not hinders other businesses.

It does not benefit any business to receive more credit than it is entitled to, unless it is the intent of the proprietor to have others carry the risk of hazardous speculations or to deliberately defraud. Credit is organized for the purpose of preventing such abuses.

Let us look at the other side of the credit coin. When a business furnishes goods or services to its customers and does not receive cash in return at the time of the transaction, it reverses its position from being a debtor and becomes the *creditor*. The business must now demand the same safeguards from its customers that it has been required to supply as a debtor.

For instance, in a simple transaction a sale is made to the point of receiving cash or something equivalent thereto to complete the transaction. The customer says "charge it" and prepares to walk off with a purchase. At this critical point the inexperienced in business may make any one of a number of common errors:

1. Failing to realize the cost of a credit transaction in contrast to cost of a cash transaction. Credit transactions result in several costs, such as the cost of tied-up capital, bookkeeping, postage, stationery, and collection. More profit is required to pay such expense.

2. Permitting goods to leave business premises without assurance of satisfactory paying "habits" and financial responsibility of customer.

3. Failing to have a clear understanding with the customer as to price or exact terms of payment expected.

4. Being too afraid of offending the customer to ask questions the seller is entitled to have answered.

5. Failing to realize that a charge sale is not a completed transaction. Until full payment is received, there is always some shadow of doubt as to the consummation of the transaction.

6. Failing to record the charge sale on the books of the business, or in being unprepared with proper billing procedure, follow-up, and collection routine.

The importance of this list is not to be minimized. When the customer takes something of value from the business, the customer may be exchanging something of *less* value — his indefinite promise to pay. The hazard of loss is always present in every credit transaction and carelessness in handling often results in a financial difficulty that might otherwise have been avoided.

It is unquestionably the customer's obligation and responsibility to pay for what he or she buys. However, every person in business learns sooner or later that customers are often careless and forgetful of such obligations. Business owners are reconciled to this situation and accept, as one of the responsibilities of business, the task of being prepared to courteously and systematically remind the patron of the debt that has been incurred.

The customer may have a poor memory or may have mislaid the bill. The customer may not understand or may dispute some item charged to him or her. The bill may never have come to his or her attention, or he or she may be waiting for a statement in order to check the balance owed. Many do not have any systematic method of paying their bills. Payment may be delayed for any of a number of reasons unknown to the merchant. The merchant may never know unless he or she takes the trouble to find out. Some customers assume the attitude that it is the creditor's worry, and can be just as indifferent about paying as the merchant is about collecting.

Those more successful in business have learned to carefully avoid making minor errors in the early stages of a credit transaction. They diligently do their part by promptly and regularly submitting bills, statements, and reminders as necessary, relentlessly pursuing the collection of money that is rightfully due them.

Being aggressive in collecting does not mean rushing to a lawyer or collection agency, nor indulging in the very hazardous practice of threatening legal action. Such last-resort measures can usually be avoided, and should be. Patience, courtesy, and firmness, intelligently and persistently applied, will generally accomplish faster and better results.

In dealing with the retail buying public, businesspeople realize that not everyone has a business-trained mind. Some have a mistaken viewpoint on credit that needs to be corrected. Some merchants extend credit so generously that customers are misled as to proper procedure in paying bills (a practice which makes it more difficult for other merchants who want to operate on a sound businesslike policy).

There may be the need to do some polite educational work, particularly if the customer shows resentment when asked to pay what is due. It may be necessary to explain, in the simplest way, the proper use of credit by both buyer and seller and the effects of its misuse on the merchant's business. The merchant has bought and paid for the goods sold to the customer, and also bought and paid for the replacement stock while waiting for the customer to pay. The goods were reasonably priced and a good value to the customer. If cash had been paid at the time of purchase, the small profit from the sale would already have gone to pay for some of the business operating expense. If the bill is not paid, it will require the profits of a great many such sales to make up the loss to the merchant.

By withholding payment, the customer is making it more difficult for the merchant to continue to give good values. The money thus tied up, combined with what other customers owe, is needed to operate the business. To borrow additional capital means an added expense in interest charges.

As a matter of fact, when the customer does not pay as agreed upon, the merchant is forced to take on the function of a bank lending money (equivalent) to the customer, which the customer is using to finance his own needs.

Conveying such facts in a friendly talk or in a courteous letter will frequently accomplish the desired results, and when customers see that a businessperson has a firm policy governing credit sales, they will usually cooperate with the seller.

Credit is of great value to business when its rules are known and adhered to. Like a complicated machine, it is not to be fooled with if one does not know how to operate it.

Credit as an adjunct to business is strictly impersonal. It is never asked for, or given, on the basis of personal favor or because of friendship. A good way to lose a customer or a friend is to have the customer or friend owe you money that is past due.

19
Conclusion

Managing a new enterprise or other small business can be a great challenge to an individual or to a team of compatible managers. The manager of a small business must be adaptable to the many challenges he or she is certain to face. He or she must often perform many tasks that may not be enjoyed in order to get the job done (such as sweeping the floor at the close of business) and to ensure the smooth functioning of the business. To survive the vicissitude of competition in an uncertain economy means that the manager of the new enterprise must have knowledge and experience in many areas, ranging from accounting to production to marketing to financing to managing others, and must master the special techniques and knowledge base of a particular industry. A career in small business or in the creation of a new enterprise can be very satisfying to those who are happy in this environment of hard work and multifaceted challenges, and for those who relish responsibility and leadership.

Index

MELLEN STUDIES IN BUSINESS